Classic Restaurants of Indianapolis

JEFFREY S. KAMM

AMERICAN PALATE

Published by American Palate
A Division of The History Press
Charleston, SC
www.historypress.net

First published 2016

Manufactured in the United States

ISBN 978.1.46711.848.4

Library of Congress Control Number: 2016944045

Notice: The information in this book is true and complete to the best of our knowledge. It is offered without guarantee on the part of the author or The History Press. The author and The History Press disclaim all liability in connection with the use of this book.

CONTENTS

Contents

PREFACE

Indianapolis often gets a bad rap as being a bland food city. Located just down from the alpha city of Chicago and all its culinary delights, it's easy to see why the "Home of Wonderbread" often is overlooked. Granted, much of this is self-inflicted, as many visitors can drive down mile after mile of automobile-oriented strip development and see the endless supply of chain restaurants serving up the same fare one can find in Sand Diego, California, or Bangor, Maine. This has not always been the case. For the past two years, I have had the privilege of writing articles for a history-oriented website in Indianapolis. My focus mainly has been places of leisure, such as restaurants, nightclubs, movie theaters and hotels. One thing I have noticed is that when I write about a long-standing local restaurant that is no longer with us, it brings out many comments and personal stories. People are drawn to unique experiences they have encountered over the years. These memories help define a sense of place and pride for the city in which they hail. People enjoy a unique dining experience despite what the modern world has programmed them to accept.

Indianapolis exists strictly by design. There was no navigable waterway that would have drawn settlers or any abundant natural resource to draw industry. The area was largely flat and swampy. In fact, the original Native Americans considered the area a common hunting ground for tribes and opted to settle in other areas. Shortly after achieving statehood, leaders desired a capital city that would be centrally located and chose the area at the convergence of the White River and Fall Creek. The state's fathers

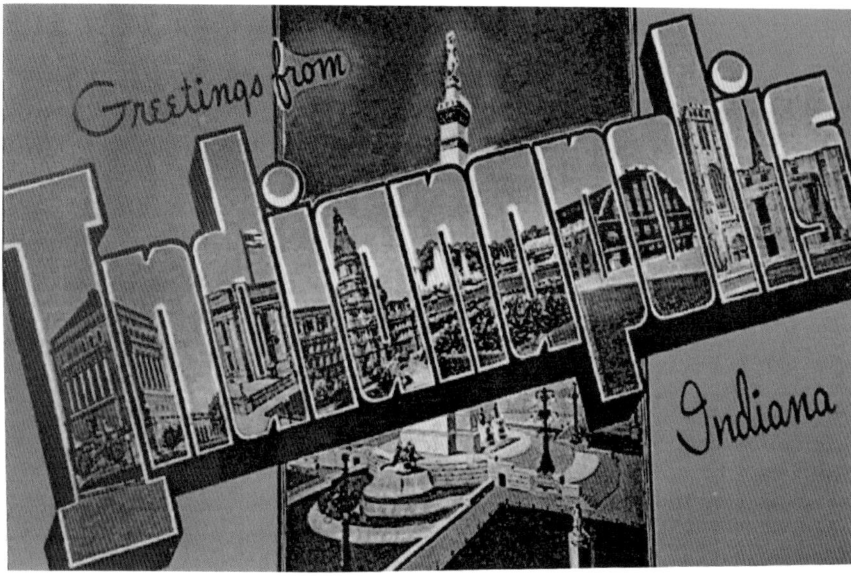

Welcome to Indianapolis! Landmarks on this postcard include the Indiana War Memorial, Federal Post Office and Courthouse, Marion County Courthouse (demolished), Garfield Sunken Gardens, Hinkle Fieldhouse, Scottish Rite Cathedral (Freemasons) and United States Naval Armory. *Courtesy of Jeff Kamm.*

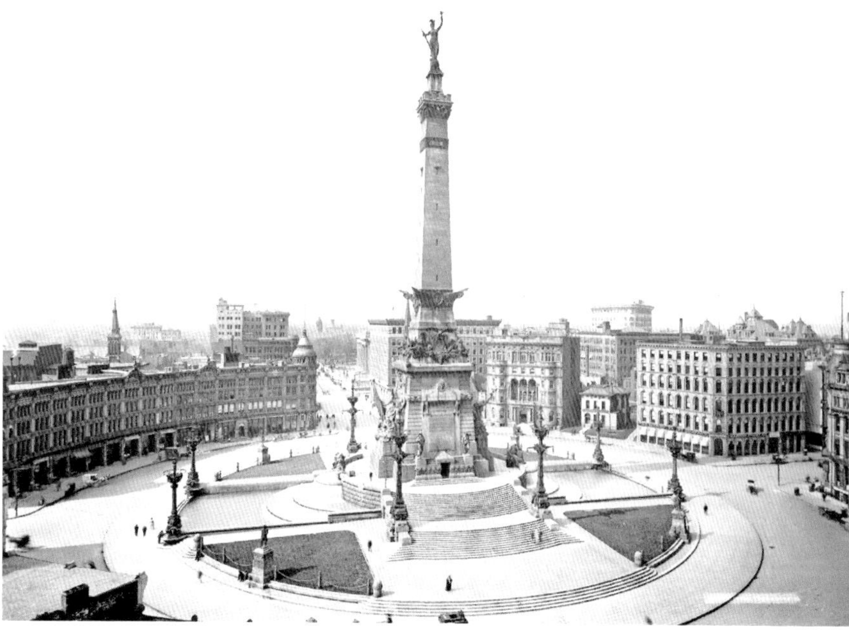

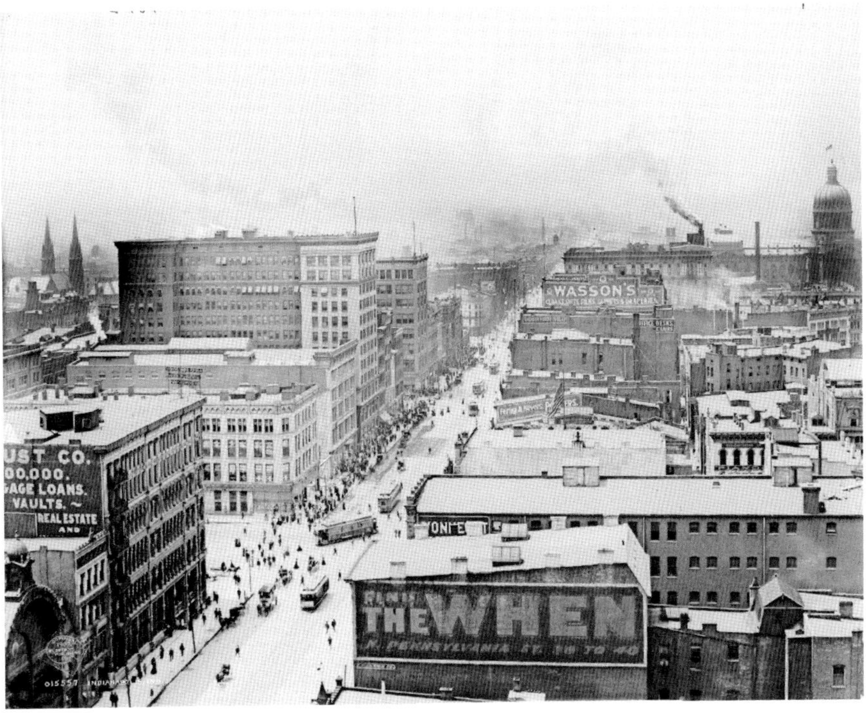

The buildings in this shot of Washington Street looking west would date this photo between 1905 and 1908. L.S. Ayres is shown completed, but the massive Barnes and Thornburg Building has yet to be constructed. L.S. Ayres was the most lavish department store in Indianapolis and featured eight floors of retail and an elegant tearoom. In the 1950s, Ayres began constructing outlets in suburban shopping centers across the state. This led to a decline in the downtown store, which closed in 1992. No trace of L.S. Ayres remains today, as it was absorbed by the Macy's chain. The massive Thomas building at mid-left was destroyed by a fire in 1973 that started in the neighboring Grant Building. Washington Street served as the major retail corridor in the city through the 1960s. *Courtesy of the Library of Congress.*

Opposite, bottom: This image of Monument Circle would predate 1925. None of the visible buildings is standing these days. The lavish English Hotel on the far left is considered one of the most notable architectural losses in the city. The building met its demise back in 1949 to make way for a rather bland J.C. Penney Store. That store closed in the early 1980s. Today, the building has been converted to offices. *Courtesy of the Library of Congress.*

chose renowned city planner Alexander Rolston to plot the land. Rolston was so enthused by the prospects of this made-from-scratch state capital that he reduced the original plan from four square miles to just one. The first New Year's celebration was held in the Wyatt Tavern, a boardinghouse that provided meals in 1822. The population was fewer than two thousand. The fledgling city would limp along for the next twenty years.

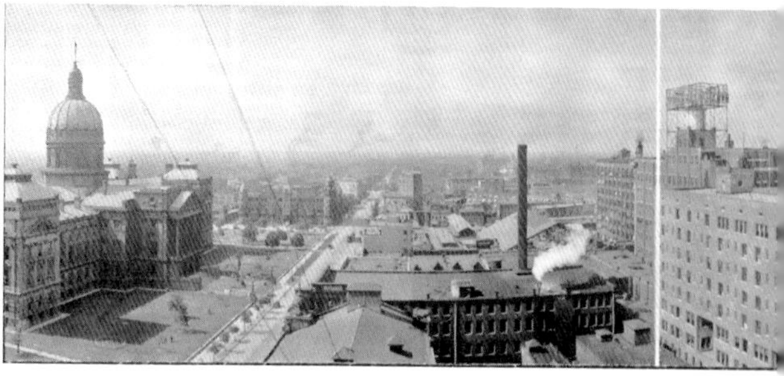

Right: These panoramic shots were taken from atop the Lincoln Hotel at the intersection of Kentucky Avenue, Illinois Street and Washington Street. The Lincoln served the city for many years and became a part of the Sheraton chain of hotels in the 1950s. The hotel's fortunes had turned by the 1960s as newer suburban hotels came into favor. The Lincoln closed in 1968. The building was imploded among much fanfare in 1973 to make way for Merchants Plaza. *Courtesy of the Library of Congress.*

Opposite: This postcard from the turn of the century shows what a typical restaurant in Indianapolis looked like at the time. The "dairy lunch" served as the fast food of the early twentieth century. Customers would order simple dishes from the counter and take them back to the seating area. Oftentimes, the seating would be single seats to discourage loitering and socializing. This establishment is true to the definition, featuring a cafeteria line along one wall. Seating consists of school desks. *Courtesy of Jeff Kamm.*

After a botched canal project that bankrupted the state, the city finally began to take off when the railroad came to town in 1847. Due to its strategic location, Indianapolis became a crossroads. The first Union Station was established here in 1853 serving all the lines converging on the city. The station was replaced in 1888 with the grand Romanesque structure that remains to this day. During this time, many hotels developed to serve different classes of travelers along Illinois Street. A strong saloon culture evolved.

By the 1920s, the automobile had begun to creep its way into the hearts of city residents, and Indianapolis served as a major manufacturing hub, rivaling even Detroit, prior to the Great Depression. During this time, a new concept of restaurant evolved. Cafeterias began popping up around the city. These restaurants featured a long counter where diners could make their selections of the items of the day. This allowed meals to be served in a quick and orderly fashion. This style of restaurant remains popular to this day. By the 1930s, another new concept had begun turning up: a restaurant where one could pull in and be served his meal in a car!

The Great Depression and food rationing in World War II limited the development of restaurants. By the 1950s, people felt liberated and were ready to celebrate their newfound wealth and prosperity. This was the heyday of the supper club. These were a one-stop shop for an evening of entertainment. You could arrive early, enjoy a lavish meal and then be entertained. These boozy and decadent rooms were often found in old

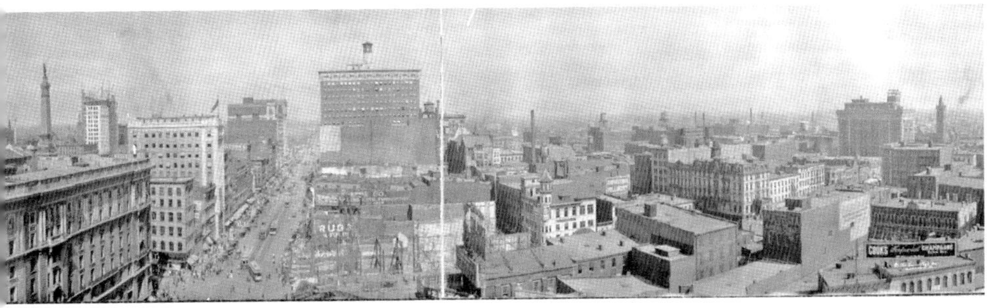

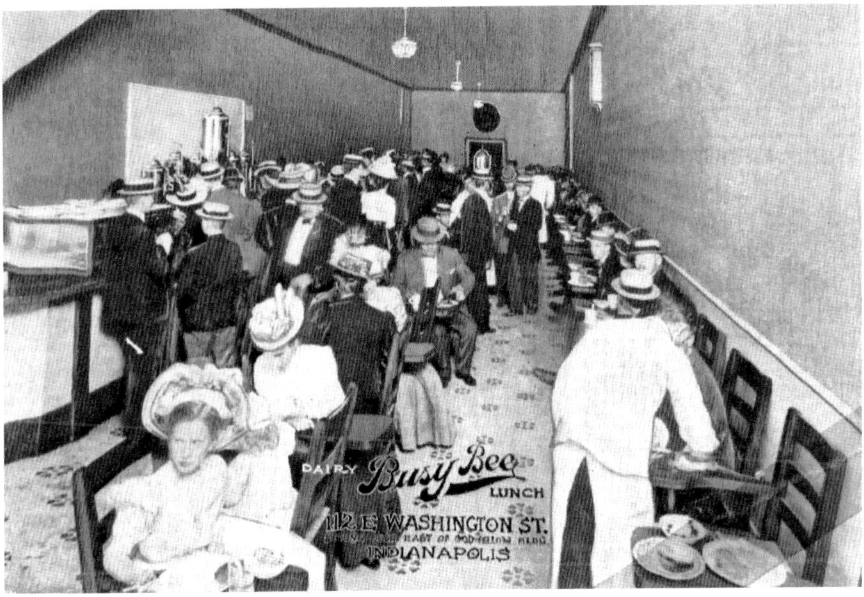

Victorian houses lining North Meridian Street. While Mom and Dad had a nice evening out, the teenagers took to the streets, creating a strong cruising culture. Drive-in restaurants would vie for attention, some offering movies or live disc jockeys. Aside from this, the roadside diner was in its heyday, and many could be found on the highways coming into the city.

By the late 1960s, things had begun to change. The once swanky clubs along Meridian Street devolved into lairs of illegal activities as the nightclub acts moved along to newer motor hotels on the outskirts of the city. People bolted from the inner-city neighborhoods for suburban cul-de-sacs. Cruising was no longer the "in thing" for teenagers, and national fast-food franchises featuring drive-through windows took over the market drive-ins once served. Strips of chain retail and dining developed along wide boulevards such as West Thirty-Eighth Street, East Eighty-Second Street and U.S. 31

on the south side. As independent restaurant owners retired or went under, Indianapolis was stripped of much of its culinary identity.

The purpose of this book is not to bash the city or its residents for allowing this bland culture to develop. Today, the landscape is slowly changing. People are rediscovering the inner city as a place to live again. Areas along Massachusetts Avenue, Virginia Avenue and North College Avenue teem with independent startups promising fresh ingredients and unique entrées. Even tired strips that once housed chain eateries have been rediscovered by entrepreneurs, many of them first-generation immigrants who open restaurants offering tastes from afar. Hopefully, by recalling what has been lost and what still remains, people will be reminded of the reward of living in a vibrant and unique community.

Chapter 1

LEGENDS THAT STAND THE TEST OF TIME

St. Elmo's Steakhouse

Even if you've never traveled to Indianapolis, you might be familiar with a "saintly" steakhouse on Illinois Street that has been serving up massive chops and fiery shrimp cocktails since 1902. Today, there is no shortage of high-end steakhouses and a promise of more to come, but locals and visitors alike still line up for a table or seat at the legendary bar.

The restaurant began as a much smaller operation consisting of the current front room and bar. Founded by Joe Stahr, the restaurant owes its namesake to the patron saint of sailors. In 1946, the restaurant changed hands. Brothers Sam and Ike Roth purchased the already popular dining establishment. Shortly thereafter, they invited their brother Harry to the partnership. The original Roth brothers left the business in 1956, leaving Harry to fend for himself. He invited longtime friend and Indianapolis bookie Izzy Rosen to come aboard as a partner. The two had grown up together and attended Manual High School. Although they possessed stark-opposite personalities—Harry being mild mannered compared to Izzy's large-and-in-charge demeanor—they turned the restaurant into an institution among downtown businessmen. The pair retired in 1986, selling the wildly popular restaurant to current owner, Stephen Huse.

A testament to the quality of the restaurant was its ability to survive the dark days of the 1960s and '70s, when downtown was going through a steep decline. Fortunes were changing for the city in 1995, when the Circle Centre

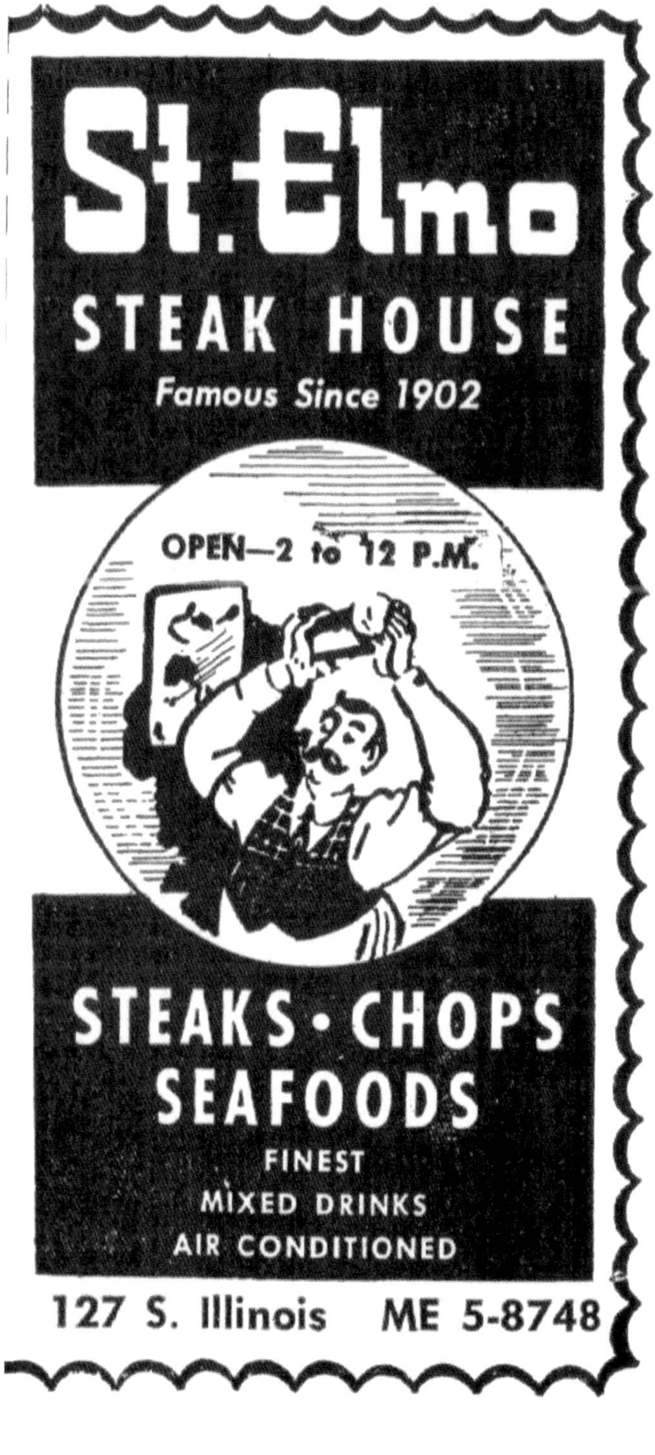

Left: A vintage ad from the 1960s promoting St. Elmo's Steakhouse. St. Elmo's advertised heavily in visitor guides during this era and became a go-to stop for visitors attending meetings and events in the Circle City. Perhaps this reputation helped it to survive the era of downtown decline in the 1960s and '70s. *Courtesy of the Indiana State Library.*

Opposite, top: This is how St. Elmo's appeared throughout the 1980s. The building was "enhanced" by wood paneling and a false roofline. The result was not particularly inviting. By 1995, the façade had been fully renovated, and the long-covered windows were opened to allow patrons to interact with street life. The popular steakhouse has since taken over the neighboring buildings to the south, along with the upper floors. *Courtesy of the Library of Congress.*

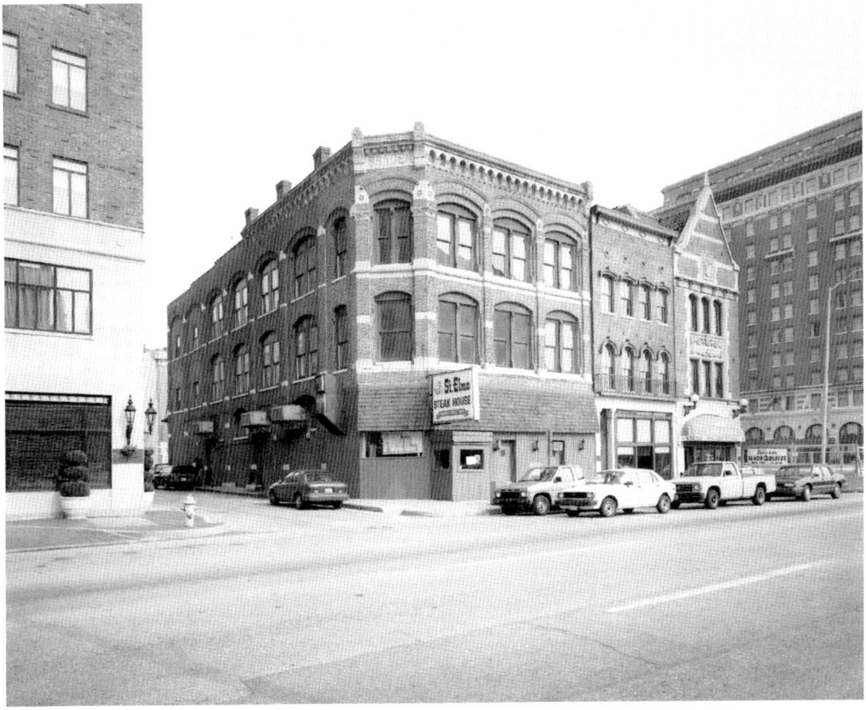

Right: St. Elmo's as it appears today. Sister restaurant Harry and Izzy's is located on the far end of the block. Harry and Izzy's offers many of the same steaks as St. Elmo's alongside an expanded menu. The famous shrimp cocktail is available at both restaurants. *Courtesy of Jeff Kamm.*

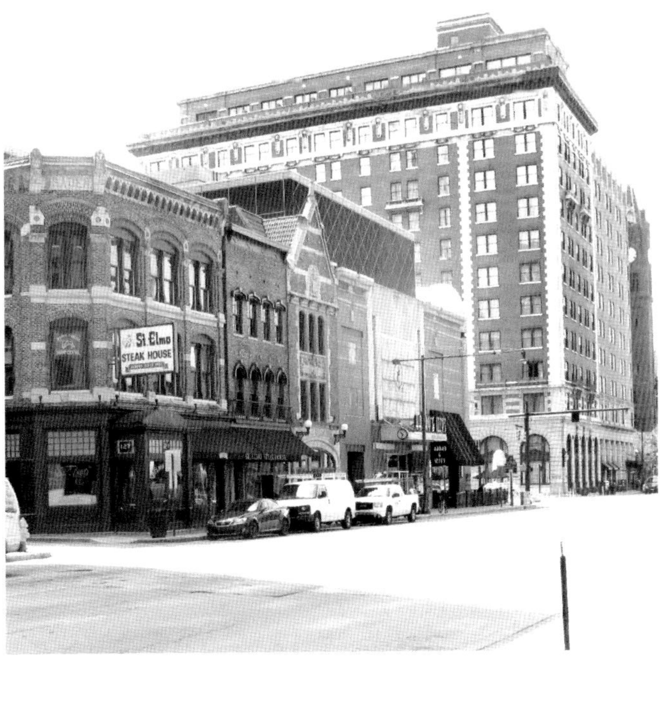

Mall opened. St. Elmo's suddenly found itself surrounded by competing upscale restaurants. Not to be outdone, the facilities have been greatly expanded over the years and now include space on the upper floors. In 2007, a sister restaurant opened near the famous location. Harry and Izzy's owes its namesake to the colorful duo who guided St. Elmo's for over thirty years. The newer eatery offers a more diverse menu, with dishes beyond the scope of carnivores. The concept has proven so successful that locations have opened on the north side and at the Indianapolis International Airport.

A Battle of the Saints

They say imitation is the sincerest form of flattery. Thirty years ago, there were two candidates vying for supreme bovine deity in Indianapolis. It was a battle of the patron saints of soldiers and sailors a mere block away from the monument that pays tribute to both. Although St. Elmo's proved victorious, many have fond memories of another saint in the former St. Moritz Steakhouse.

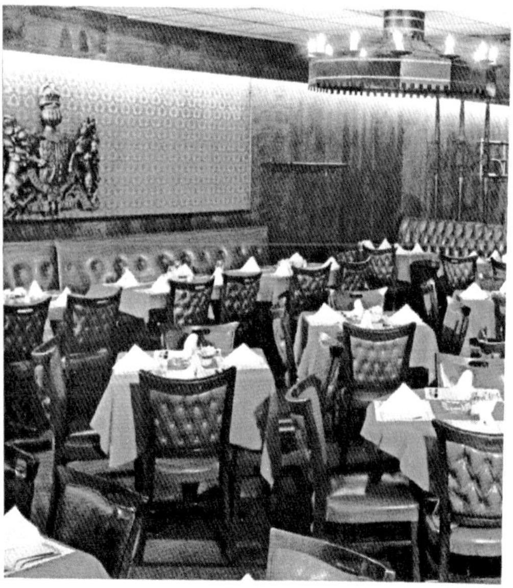

St. Moritz Steak House

44 N. PENNSYLVANIA ST.
1 Block East of Monument Circle

Complete Menu

Open Hearth Charcoal Broiler

Favorite Cocktails

We Honor All Credit Cards

Our new dining room will provide additional seating for 100 and accomodate evening meeting groups or banquets.

Serving Luncheons from 11: A.M. and Dinner til 12 Midnight

For Dinner Reservations . . .

Call 637-9666

St. Moritz boasted number two billing among Indianapolis steakhouses. The restaurant relocated to swankier digs in the 1960s in the reconstructed Vincent-Pierce block, which replaced one of the oldest commercial structures in Indianapolis. The entire block on the west side of Pennsylvania Street was demolished in 1995 for the construction of a large parking structure. *Courtesy of the Indiana State Museum.*

Restaurants with a sixty-year shelf life are quite rare. While popular celebrities and athletes have long been a fixture at St. Elmo's, the politicians and lawyers of Indianapolis would often spend their evenings at St. Moritz Steakhouse, which was located one block east of the circle. Founded in the unlucky year of 1929 by the Zilson family on the ground floor of the Lemcke Building at 109 North Pennsylvania Street, the restaurant put up a noble fight, enduring the Great Depression, World War II and the gradual decline of downtown over the next forty years.

By 1968, the restaurant was under the stewardship of Nick Zilson, a nephew of the original owners. Under his guidance, the popular eatery moved across the street to 44 North Pennsylvania Street, near the intersection with Market. The business remained popular, often advertising itself in a tongue-in-cheek manner as the number two steakhouse in Indianapolis. It seemed as if St. Moritz would last forever as an Indianapolis legend.

But popularity did not stop the power of real estate speculators. In 1984, a massive project was proposed on the site of St. Moritz and the two historic structures to the south. The ambitious Symphony Towers were to consist of some seven hundred apartments in a forty-eight-story building, a seven-hundred-space parking structure and thirty thousand square feet of retail space. Accepting the restaurant's fate, Zilson prepared to celebrate the last day of business on July 1, 1987. Banners decorated the Swiss chalet façade, and many local movers and shakers enjoyed one last meal. Zilson told stories behind the bar, including an instance in which he was slapped by a prominent politician after cutting off his drinks for the evening. The two eventually reconciled and became friends.

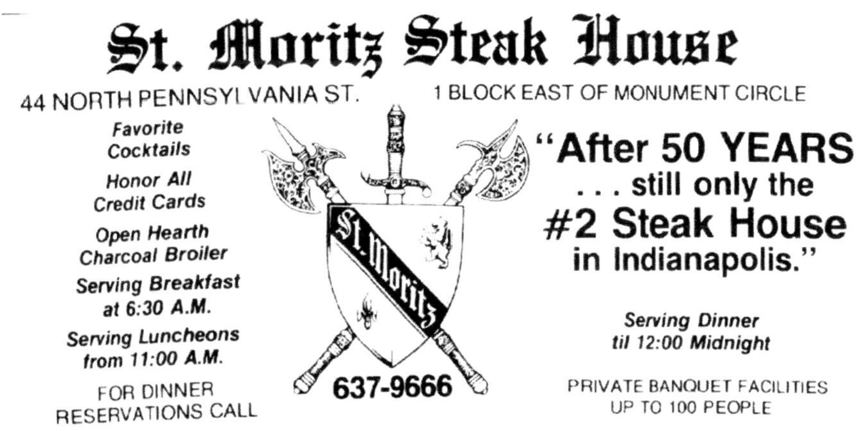

This tongue-in-cheek ad from 1980 promotes the St. Moritz Steakhouse. *Courtesy of the Indiana State Museum.*

The plan for Symphony Towers ended up bursting with the rest of the real estate market in the late 1980s. The buildings intended to be cleared sat in various states of disrepair for nearly a decade until they were demolished in 1994 for one of the city's many bland parking structures. Zilson went on to manage J. Whit's restaurant in the Lockerbie Marketplace until it closed in 1991. He passed away in 2008 at the age of seventy-nine.

Shapiro's Delicatessen

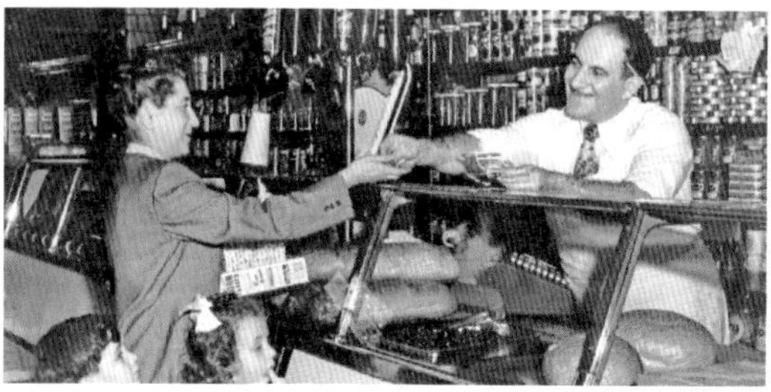

Shapiro's patriarch Max Shapiro hands change to a customer in 1950. The customer is identified as Mrs. Frania Kaplan. The Kaplans were the first Jewish family to relocate to Indianapolis in the years following World War II. *Courtesy of the Indiana Historical Society.*

The Jewish population in Indianapolis is quite small, making up only around 1 percent of the total population. Despite these relatively small numbers, the Jewish community is entrenched in the city's history. The first wave of Jewish immigrants began arriving in the early 1850s. They were primarily of German origin and served as clothiers, shopkeepers and retailers. Closer to the turn of the century, a second wave of Jewish emigrants came from east Europe and Russia. One of these, Louis Shapiro, created an Indianapolis institution.

Louis Shapiro arrived in Indianapolis in 1901. By 1903, he had started a pushcart business, selling groceries door-to-door in the Jewish enclave located just south of downtown. In 1905, Louis opened a grocery store at 808 South Meridian Street. As time went on, the operation transitioned from grocery to restaurant. After Prohibition ended, the establishment began serving beer, and demand increased for sandwiches piled high with kosher meats.

By mid-century, the city's Jewish population had largely scattered to the affluent north side of the city, and the restaurant evolved into a popular lunch spot, particularly with employees of nearby Eli Lilly. After Louis Shapiro passed away in 1950, his son Max took over and gradually expanded the store. By the 1980s, the south side landmark was nearly four times the size of the original operation, and a second location was opened on West Eighty-

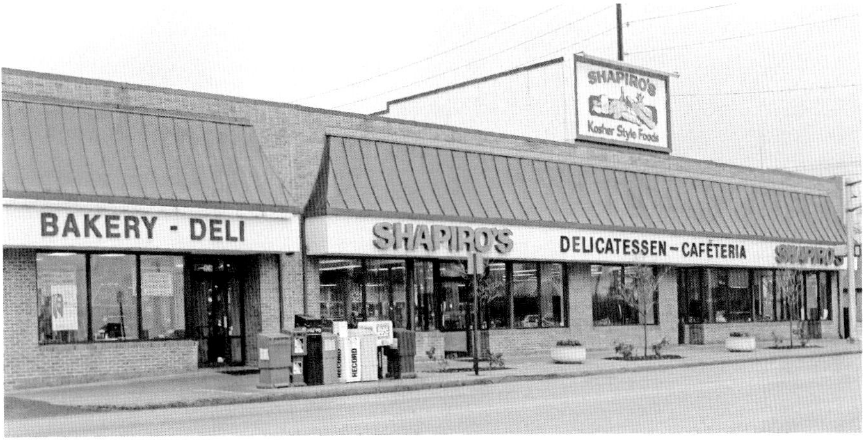

Shapiro's as it appears today on South Meridian Street, providing Indianapolis with authentic kosher foods as it has since 1905. The restaurant also features outposts at Keystone at the Crossing and at the Indianapolis International Airport. *Courtesy of Jeff Kamm.*

Sixth Street across from St. Vincent Hospital. Around this time, a successor to lead the family business was needed. Max, not having any children, selected his nephew Brian to come aboard.

Under Brian's leadership, the business has continued to thrive, despite setbacks and changing times. In 2002, a Carmel location replaced the West Eighty-Sixth Street location. In 2003, a fire at the downtown location shut down the business for nearly three months. These days, the downtown location remains an Indianapolis landmark. Nationally televised sporting events often feature footage of Shapiro's employees stacking their famous sandwiches with piles of corned beef or pastrami. In 2008, Shapiro's flew into the brand-new Indianapolis International Airport terminal, which features many local eateries. The Carmel location was recently replaced with a store at the upscale Fashion Mall at Keystone. To this day, a sign appears near the deli counter with the founder's motto: "Cook Good; Serve Generously; Price Modestly; People will come." With this consistent pledge to quality and caring family stewardship, Shapiro's should continue to be a go-to name in Indianapolis dining.

Hollyhock Hill

Prior to the days of fast-paced life filled with drive-through windows and grab-and-go meals, people enjoyed sitting down with their families at home for leisurely meals. As a result, many early restaurants tried to emulate a Sunday dinner at Grandma's house. Indianapolis is lucky enough to have a couple examples of such establishments in existence today. One of these is Hollyhock Hill.

Hollyhock Hill traces its root all the way back to 1928. That's when Mr. V.D. Vincent began opening his country cottage on the northern fringes of Marion County for special family-style dinners to customers of his In Town Restaurant. Back then, North College Avenue was a lonely outpost, far from the urban bustle of the capital city. The name is derived from the secluded nature of the cabin, along with the hollyhocks on the premises. Mr. Vincent operated the restaurant until selling to Mr. and Mrs. Hubert Kelso in 1947. Under the Kelsos' watch, the restaurant expanded to seat over 150 patrons. Mr. Kelso was considered an industry leader and served as president of the Indiana Restaurant Association. During the Kelsos' stewardship, the restaurant served many politicians, race fans and even stars of the stage and screen such as Tim Conway, who came to perform in the Starlight Musicals at nearby Butler University.

In 1958, the Kelsos hired a young Jay Snyder to be a "yard boy." His tasks included maintaining the property and grounds. After a time, Mr. Snyder would be called on to help out in the kitchen during a pinch. It was during this time that he met another employee named Barbara, whom he would later marry. Through the years, Mr. Snyder learned the business and eventually became a stockholder in 1972, when the restaurant incorporated. When the Kelsos finally retired in 1992, Mr. and Mrs. Snyder assumed ownership and still operate the restaurant today.

These days, the restaurant remains extremely popular for special occasions and other celebrations. The formula has remained tried and true over the

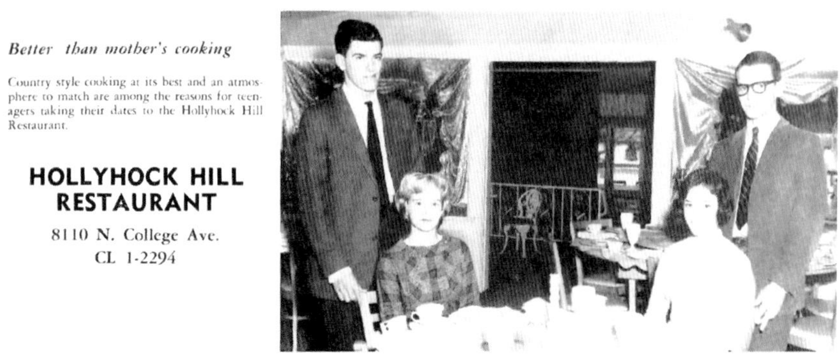

North Central students await a special night out at Hollyhock Hill. *Courtesy Indianapolis–Marion County Library.*

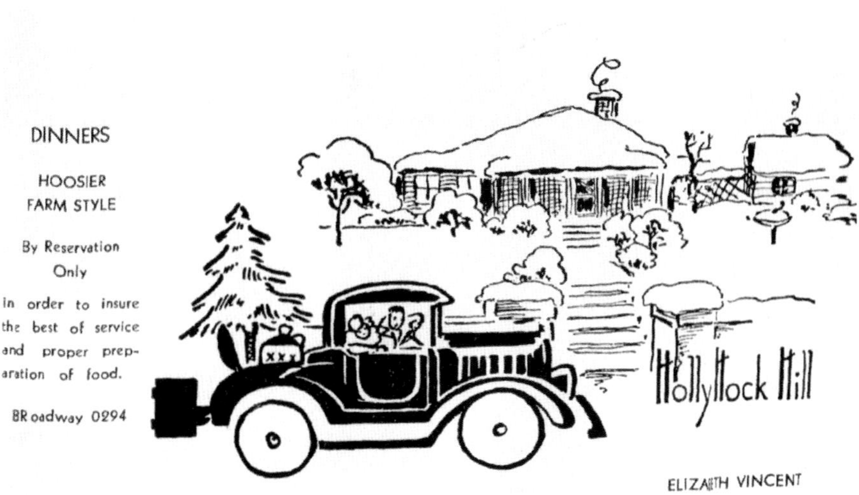

This postcard from the 1930s depicts the homey nature of Hollyhock Hill. At the time, the restaurant was a destination in a rural area of Marion County. *Courtesy of Jeff Kamm.*

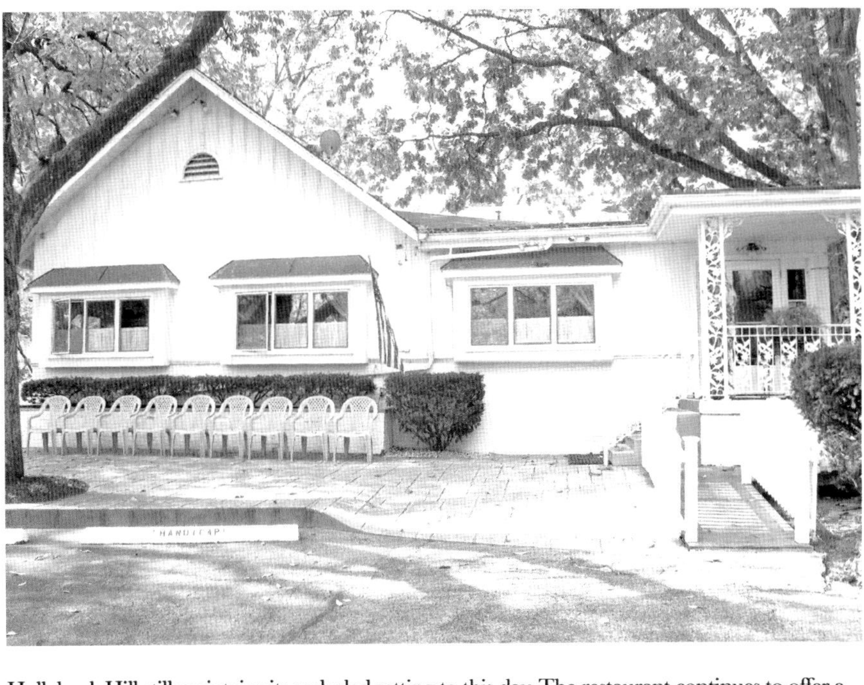

Hollyhock Hill still maintains its secluded setting to this day. The restaurant continues to offer a homey atmosphere reminiscent of a Sunday dinner at Grandma's. *Courtesy of Jeff Kamm.*

years, with heaping portions of fried chicken served family style alongside mashed potatoes, buttered corn, green beans and homemade biscuits. Aside from the chicken, some popular menu items include jumbo fried shrimp, several fish options and steaks. Despite increasing competition and the decreasing attention spans of diners, the restaurant remains popular due to its home-like atmosphere and impeccable service. The location still maintains a secluded "cabin in the woods"–like atmosphere despite the growth of the city, and one can imagine the experience emulates what diners experienced during the first half of the twentieth century.

The Iron Skillet

Much like Hollyhock Hill, the Iron Skillet specializes in family-style chicken dinners in a rustic setting; in fact, you might notice the service and accompanying sides are similar, from the wedge salad to the unique rotating tray of sundae toppings. This is for good reason, as this west side institution was founded in 1956 by Mr. Charles Kelso, brother of Hubert Kelso of Hollyhock Hill.

The building that houses the restaurant has an even greater history. The large house was built by a German immigrant named August Wacker. At the time, Wacker had purchased ninety acres surrounding the area of West Thirtieth Street and Cold Springs Road. A pioneer in suburban development, Wacker subdivided the land and sold around forty homes, built new streets and established trolley service in the area. Shortly after the turn of the century, the large home served as the clubhouse for the newly formed Highland Country Club, which once occupied the space that is now Coffin Golf Course.

Mr. and Mrs. Charles Kelso purchased the property in 1956, converting it into a restaurant. The Kelsos ran the restaurant until 1996. Upon retirement, Mr. Kelso sold the business to Mr. Ronald Torr. Mr. Torr has kept the tradition and atmosphere of the restaurant alive as people flock there for the familiar family dinners served with salads, sides and a delicious homemade onion soup. Aside from the fried chicken, another popular choice is the combo dinner that features fried shrimp, a small beef tenderloin and the famous fowl. Mr. Torr takes great pride in being an independent, non-chain establishment and maintains a staff of long-term employees. Due to the great food and proximity to the famed Indianapolis Motor Speedway, the

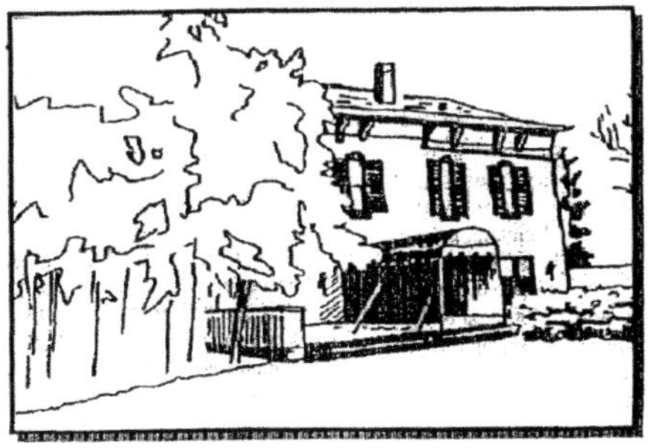

The Iron Skillet

2489 W. 30th Street
Indianapolis, Indiana 46222
317-923-6353
www.ironskillet.net

FAMILY STYLE DINING
Since
1953

Serving all Year
Wednesday thru Saturday
5:30 P.M to 8:30 P.M.
Sunday
12:00 Noon to 7:30 P.M.

Right: This sketch portrays the stately historic farmhouse that houses the Iron Skillet. The restaurant was a clubhouse for what is now Coffin Golf Course. *Courtesy of Ron Torr.*

Below: The dining room features white tablecloths and pre-set service for a family-style meal. Entrées and sides are served on large platters and passed among diners. *Courtesy of Jeff Kamm.*

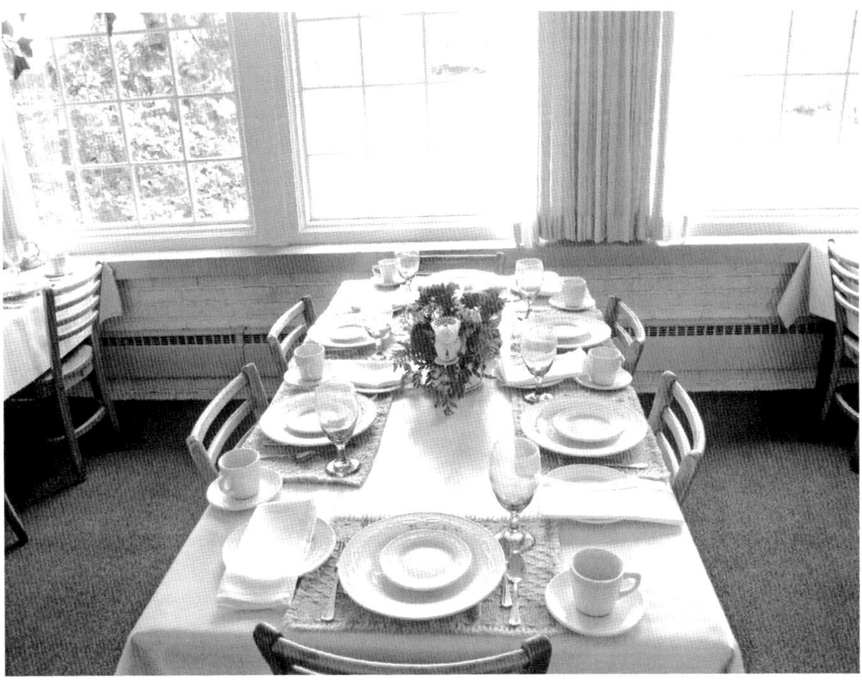

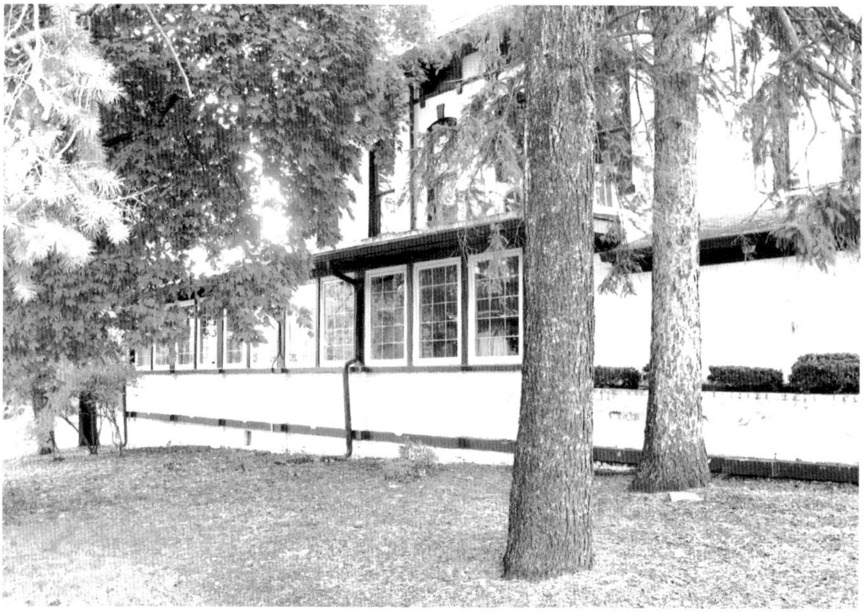

The restaurant maintains a stately presence on a bluff overlooking the White River and Coffin Golf Course. *Courtesy of Jeff Kamm.*

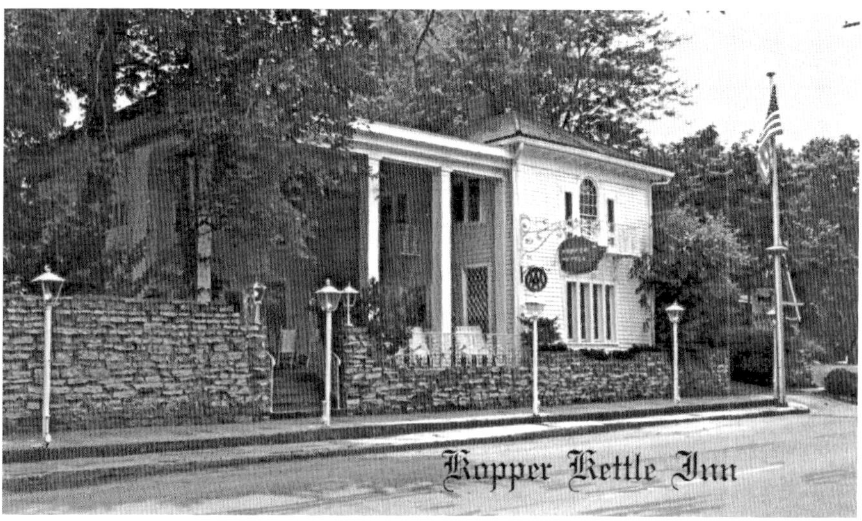

The Kopper Kettle Inn, located in Morristown, Indiana, was also owned by the Kelso family at one point. The restaurant features food and service similar to what one finds at Hollyhock Hill and the Iron Skillet. *Courtesy of Jeff Kamm.*

Iron Skillet has seen its share of famous guests through the years. Celebrities include Parnelli Jones, James Gardner, John Travolta, Carol Burnett and Ernest Borgnine. The restaurant even hosted President John F. Kennedy during his ill-fated reelection campaign in 1962.

Historic Steer-In

The spot on East Tenth Street has been occupied by a drive-in restaurant of some sort dating back to the Depression. During this time, a restaurant known as the North Pole began serving frozen custard and other dairy treats. The business remained through the 1950s, specializing in serving frozen treats during the summer months.

Things changed in 1960, when the Laughner family purchased the venture. The Laughners had been in the restaurant business since 1888 and opened the first cafeteria in Indiana. They demolished the original structure and opened the Steer-In, hoping to capitalize on the "cruising culture" of the day. Apparently, the business did not fit with the Laughners' model, and the east side hangout was sold to Harold Phillips in 1964. Under the name

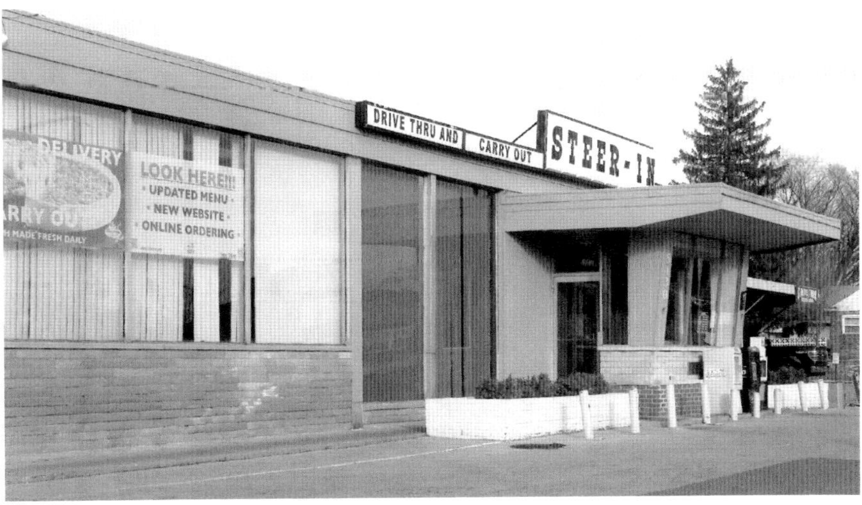

Doing business under the names of Laughner's and Harold's, the east side landmark now operates under the name the Historic Steer-In after being purchased by longtime employees. Car-hop service ended when the restaurant expanded in the 1980s, but the covered parking area gives a clue to the once popular teen hangout's past. *Courtesy of Jeff Kamm.*

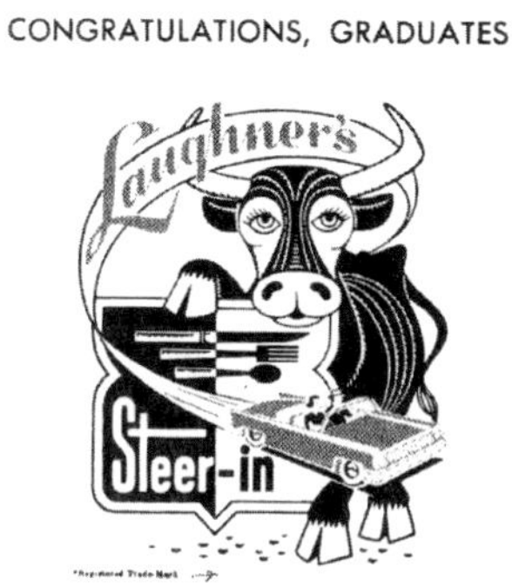

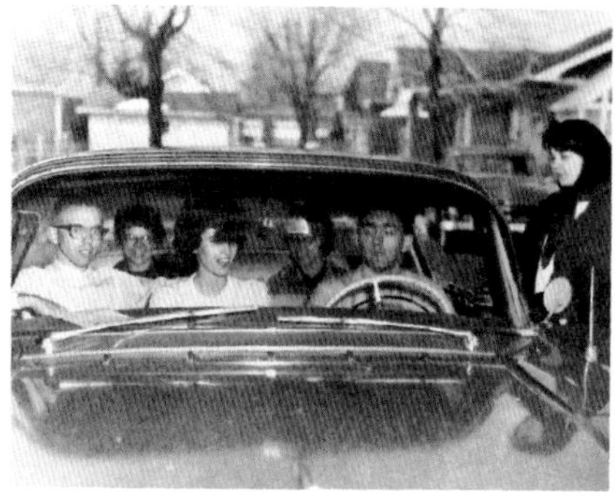

Left to right—Jim, Rita, Betty, Ilze and Don.

Tech High School students enjoy a snack at Laughner's Steer-In in the early 1960s. The drive-in would have been a hotspot for the massive east side high school's students. *Courtesy of the Indianapolis–Marion County Public Library.*

Harold's Steer-In, the restaurant became a cruising hotspot and thrived throughout the 1960s and '70s. By the 1980s, the drive-in restaurant had become a fading institution, so Phillips expanded the indoor dining area and eliminated curb service. The restaurant became known for its twenty-four-hour breakfast menu catering to the blue-collar east side shift workers.

According to the restaurant's website, the operation continued until 2007. This was when the Keher family bought the operation from Harold and changed the name to the Historic Steer-In. Today, the restaurant features several original recipes, including the "Twin Steer" hamburger. Other home-cooked items have been added, and the restaurant maintains a loyal following. It has been featured on the Food Network's *Diners, Drive-Ins and Dives* and shows no sign of slowing down.

Mug n' Bun Drive-In

Today's fast-food culture has made us accustomed to sitting in our idling cars, pulling up to a window to receive our meals and heading down the road while trying to juggle a sandwich along with the steering wheel. That hasn't always been the case, and one Indianapolis institution still clings stubbornly to a business model that many consider completely passé.

The Mug n' Bun Drive-In started serving up standard drive-in fare in the 1960s and really hasn't changed much. Located in Speedway on the far

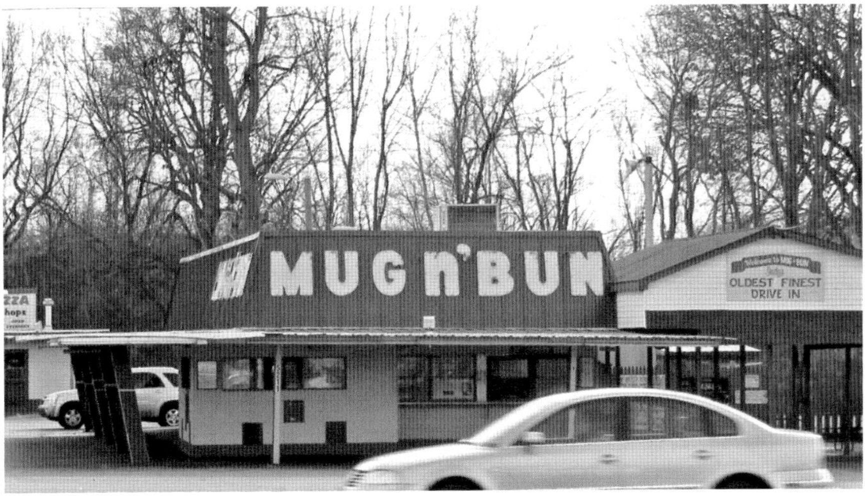

The Mug n' Bun Drive-In is a west side institution. Opening in 1960, the restaurant sits in the shadow of the Indianapolis Motor Speedway. Diners enjoy breaded tenderloin sandwiches, onion rings and homemade root beer served to them in their vehicles. *Courtesy of Jeff Kamm.*

west side, the restaurant, much like the surrounding neighborhood, delivers an unintentional dose of nostalgia. Customers pull in and park under the canopied parking area; peruse the menu conveniently painted on the side of the bright, golden building; and flip on their headlights once the decision has been made. The fare is definitely not intended for those watching their figures. Aside from the typical hamburgers and fries, menu items consist of many other delights from the fryer, such as pork tenderloins and fried shrimp and catfish. Coney dogs are another popular choice. One would be foolish if he didn't wash down these classic dishes with a mug of the sweet, lightly carbonated root beer made on-site.

The business has made some changes over the years as teenage cruising has waned. These days, the drive-in caters largely to families wanting to show their children a bit of yesteryear. For those not wanting to grasp for loose French fries lodged under the seat, a picnic area has been added so folks can escape their vehicles. An indoor dining room has recently been added so folks don't have to brave the elements on cold days. Despite these changes, Mug n' Bun remains one of the last authentic drive-in restaurants in the city.

Rathskeller Restaurant

The Rathskeller Restaurant in the historic Athenaeum is truly a survivor. The building, constructed to embrace German culture and heritage, has seen the ugliness of anti-ethnic sentiment during two world wars, the decline of downtown, the threat of demolition in the name of urban renewal and fickle fancies in dining and entertainment.

Germans have been immigrating to Indianapolis in large numbers for years, many arriving between 1848 and 1860. Prior to the First World War, it might have been difficult for one to tell the difference between Indiana and Germany. State laws were published in both English and German. Public education offered courses in both languages. At the dawn of the twentieth century, many German social clubs flourished in Indianapolis. One of these was the Turner Society. This group was founded in 1851 to foster and promote German culture. Under the guidance of the Socialer Turnverein, these groups decided to build a massive clubhouse for their activities. The group moved into its new clubhouse, dubbed Das Deutsche Haus, in 1894. The building

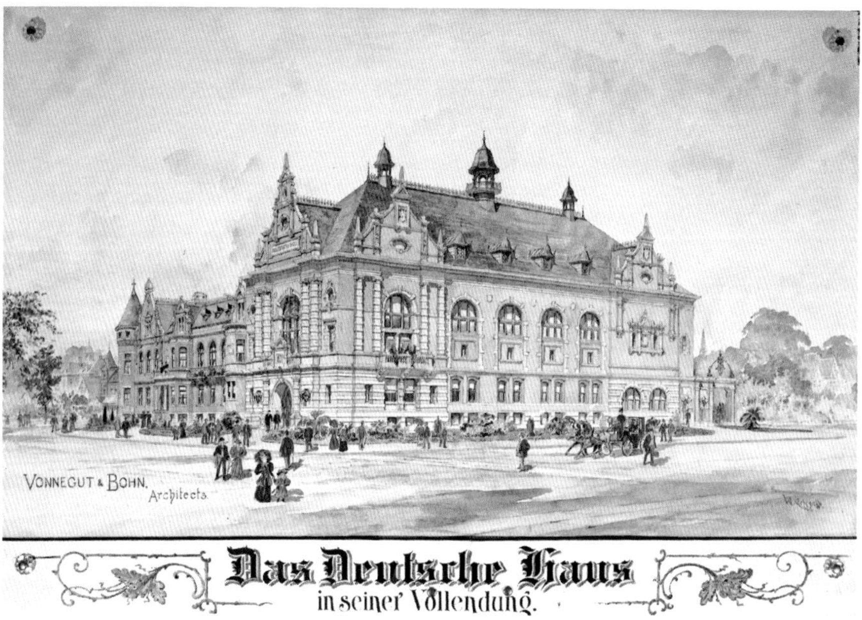

An artist's rendering of Das Deusche Haus on East Michigan Street. The architecture firm Vonnegut and Bohn was formed by Bernard Vonnegut in 1888. Vonnegut was the grandfather of author Kurt Vonnegut. The building appears much the same today as it does in this rendering. *Courtesy of the Library of Congress.*

was designed by the firm Vonnegut and Bohn, which also designed many Indianapolis landmarks. Das Deutsche Haus became the hub for all things German, housing the German-English School Society, the German-American Veterans' Society, the Socialer Turnverein Women's Club, the German Ladies' Aid Society and the Turner Building and Savings Association.

Life was good, and the society thrived until World War I. The German House became known as the Athenaeum in 1918, as many citizens adopted anti-German sentiment. This attitude would persist through World War II. The Turners survived and thrived as interest in German culture rebounded in the postwar years. The Athenaeum became the hub for many festivals and celebrations. This renewed interest likely saved the building from demolition in the 1970s, when the city demolished many historic structures for parking and ill-advised urban renewal projects.

The Athenaeum has been lovingly restored throughout the years. Guests will notice the elaborate brickwork and stained-glass windows. In 1991, the building was acquired by the newly formed Athenaeum Foundation. The organization has been able to secure donations over the years to ensure that

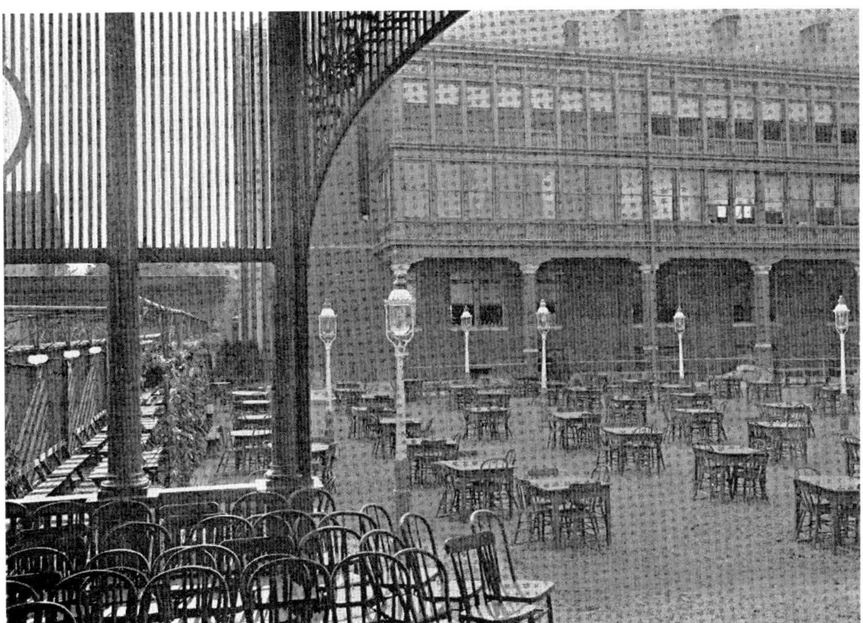

The outdoor beer garden at the Rathskeller as it appeared in the 1920s. The space appears nearly the same today; however, the tables have been replaced with long picnic tables. The beer garden is immensely popular during the summer and features live music nightly. *Courtesy of the Library of Congress.*

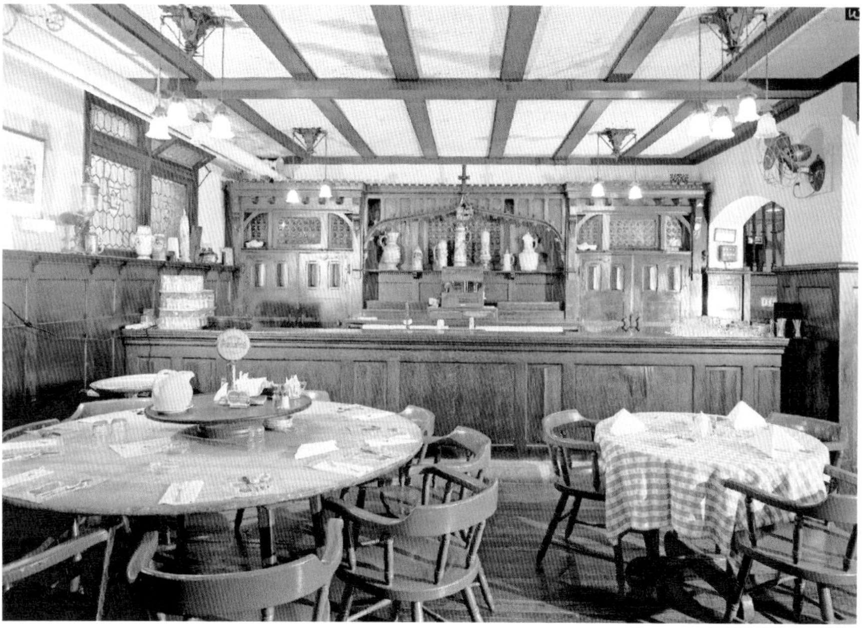

A dining room in the historic Rathskeller Restaurant in downtown Indianapolis. The building was erected during the heyday of the Turner movement. Constructed in 1893, it was originally known as Das Deutsche House but came to be known as the Athenaeum during the height of anti-German sentiment during the first world war. *Courtesy of the Library of Congress.*

the landmark is maintained for future generations to enjoy. The Rathskeller Restaurant has continuously served diners since 1894, making it the oldest restaurant in Indianapolis. Diners can choose to eat in the formal dining room or relax with sandwiches and beer in the Kellerbar. During the summer months, the outdoor beer garden is immensely popular with the ever-growing base of downtown residents. Either way, the Rathskeller and Athenaeum offer a wonderful way to bask in the history of our German heritage.

Chapter 2

GONE BUT NOT FORGOTTEN

KING COLE RESTAURANT

If you were going on a first date or celebrating an anniversary or other special occasion, what would be your go-to spot? For nearly seventy years, the answer to that question could be found at Seven North Meridian Street in a building that is to this day referred to by the name of the legendary restaurant that once occupied the basement: the King Cole.

The ten-story building at the northeast corner of Washington and Meridian Streets is noteworthy not only for its prime location but also because it was designed by Vonnegut, Bohn and Mueller, a firm started by the grandfather of famous author Kurt Vonnegut. The firm designed many Art Deco buildings, including the Indiana Bell headquarters farther up Meridian Street.

The first restaurant featured in the below-ground space opened as the Seville in 1929. By 1957, the remodeled space had been renamed the King Cole. At the opening of the King Cole, owner Max Comisar bragged about the art collection. The Dayton native purchased over thirty oil paintings to be displayed throughout the establishment, most dating back to the seventeenth and eighteenth centuries, including works by Rembrandt. He purchased these to keep with the old English theme in the formal Seville space. Large oak tables were flanked with leather-upholstered chairs. Diners were introduced to a unique technology. Phone jacks located at each table allowed businessmen to conduct important business matters over their meals.

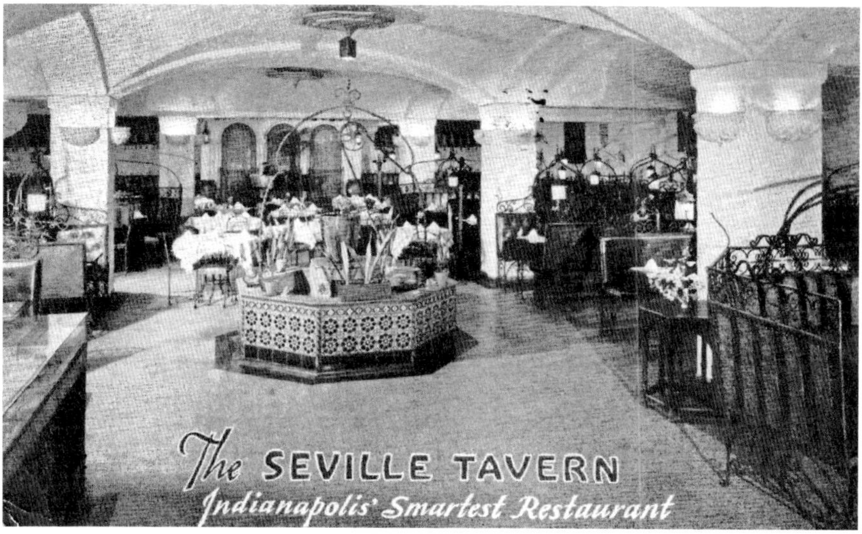

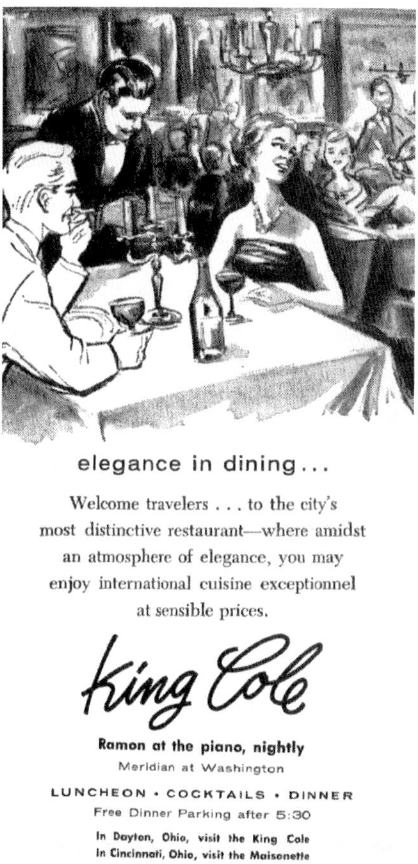

Above: The King Cole Restaurant was originally known as the Seville Tavern. After a hefty remodel in 1957, the restaurant became known as the King Cole and served the jacket-clad set until the mid-1990s. *Courtesy of Jeff Kamm.*

Left: This ad from the 1950s boasts the elegance of the King Cole Restaurant. The restaurant was apparently under the same stewardship as the famous Maisonette in Cincinnati, Ohio. *Courtesy of the Indiana State Library.*

Customers entering the restaurant were greeted by a large cooler displaying various meats from which they could select their prized cuts. Steaks and seafood would become the specialty of the house.

This was *the* destination restaurant in Indiana. The décor was intentionally stuffy. The establishment's advertising boasted that it was the best and often listed awards won throughout the years. A strict dress code requiring jackets remained in place through the 1980s. The restaurant remained popular for prom dates and anniversaries throughout the 1970s, until a bout with Legionnaire's disease in 1979 damaged its sterling reputation. The restaurant held on through the 1980s, but changing tastes in dining would bring an end to the once grand downtown destination. The sought-after French continental cuisine for which it was known became less popular. So

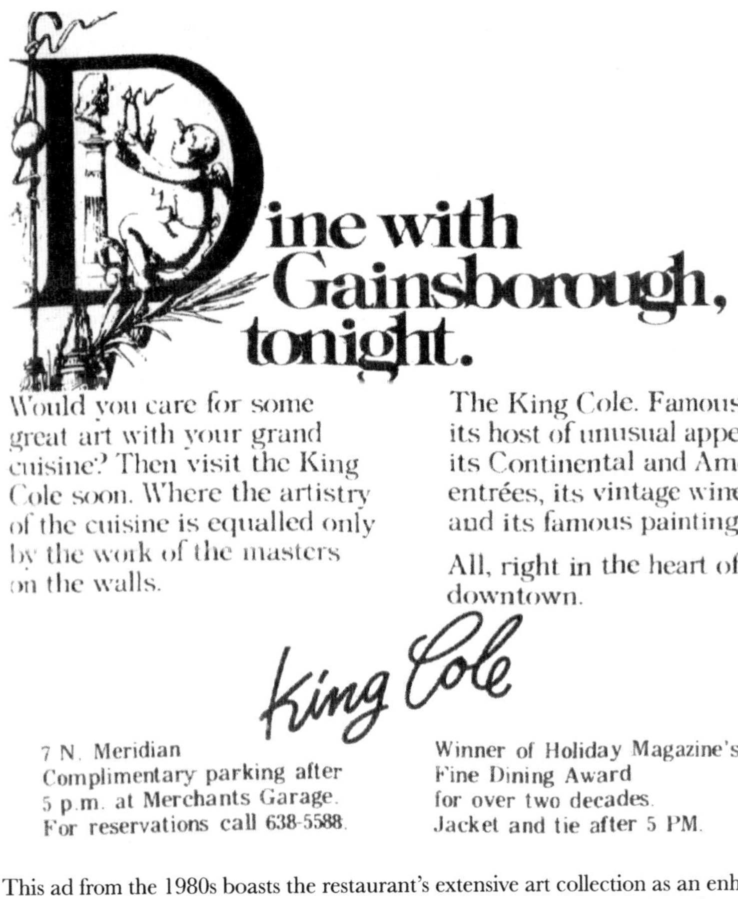

This ad from the 1980s boasts the restaurant's extensive art collection as an enhancement of the dining experience. The King Cole would have been the go-to place for special occasions. *Courtesy of the Indiana State Library.*

did the formality of service and dress that were part of the dining experience. By the 1990s, the restaurant had gone through a change in management. It ditched the strict dress code and even paired up with a local nightclub for cross promotion. New menu items featuring chicken and pasta dishes were introduced. It all proved futile, and the doors closed for good in 1994, when it became clear the changes weren't resulting in an influx of new customers.

But this would not be the end of swanky nights out at this beloved location. Nicky Blaine's cigar and martini bar took over the space in 1999. Riding the resurgence of swing music and cigar smoking popularized in the late 1990s, the bar became an immediate success—so successful, in fact, that it moved across the street to a larger space to accommodate its crowds in 2005. Today, the space sits empty, awaiting its next repurposing.

L.S. Ayres Tea Room

When one mentions lost restaurants of Indianapolis, it's hard to ignore the L.S. Ayres Tea Room. Entire books have been written on the subject. Perched on top of the most elegant department store, the tearoom served as a destination for hungry shoppers for over ninety years. During its heyday, the restaurant would be packed with people dressed in their Sunday best dining on dainty sandwiches and chicken velvet soup. Children would behave with the promise of visiting the treasure chest at the end of the meal.

The tearoom can trace its roots back to 1872. That's when Lyman S. Ayres started a dry goods business on Washington Street. Business must have been pretty good because, after several years of prosperity, Ayres constructed one of the first steel-framed buildings in the city. Construction was completed in 1905. The new department store featured three restaurants, including the tearoom.

The year 1929 proved to be a big one for the tearoom. A brand-new twelve-story addition was added to the south side of the massive department store. This doubled the retail space, adding a new men's department and seven new high-speed elevators. The new tearoom was twice the size of the old one and featured a promenade where people could gather before or after lunch. The L.S. Ayres Tea Room would continue to serve shoppers with little change for the next fifty years.

The year 1990 was an ugly time for downtown Indianapolis. By this point, both flagship department stores, L.S. Ayres and Block's, had been

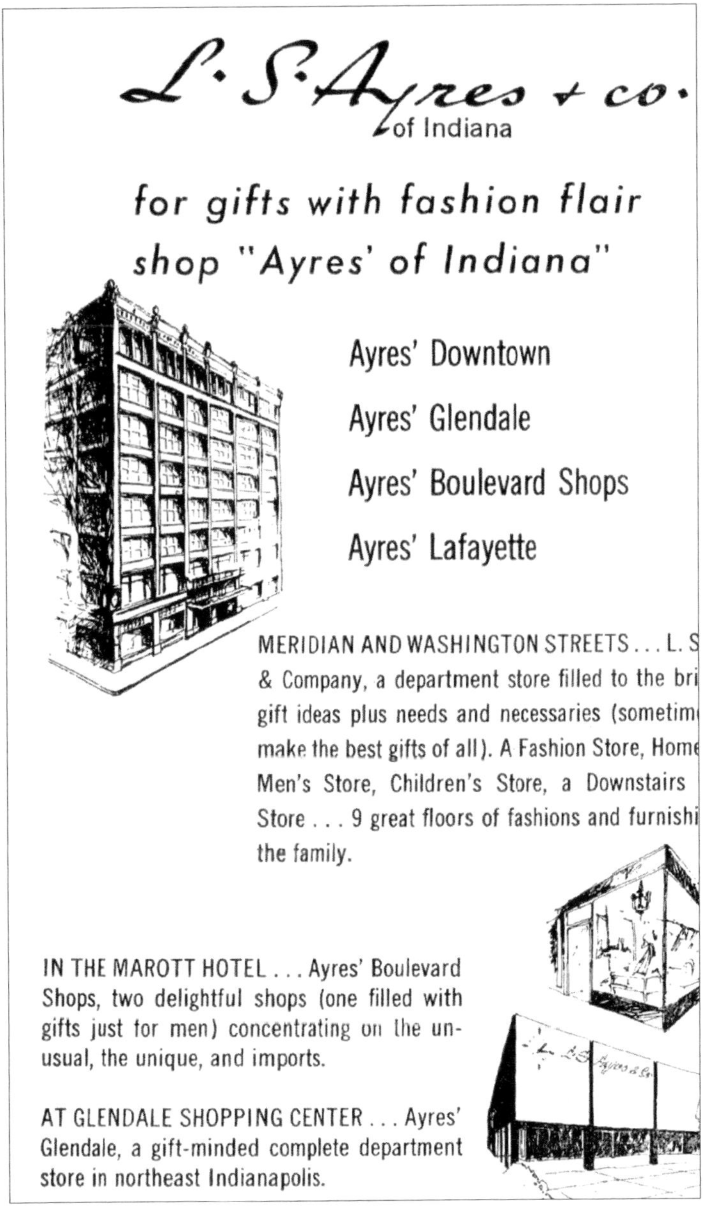

This advertisement, circa 1958, not only boasts of the mammoth downtown L.S. Ayres department store but also of a new store at Glendale Center on the northeast side and a smaller boutique at the Marott Hotel. In addition to these stores, Ayres opened a store at the Market Square Center in Lafayette, Indiana. None of these new locations featured the legendary tearoom—that was exclusive to downtown. *Courtesy of the Indiana State Library.*

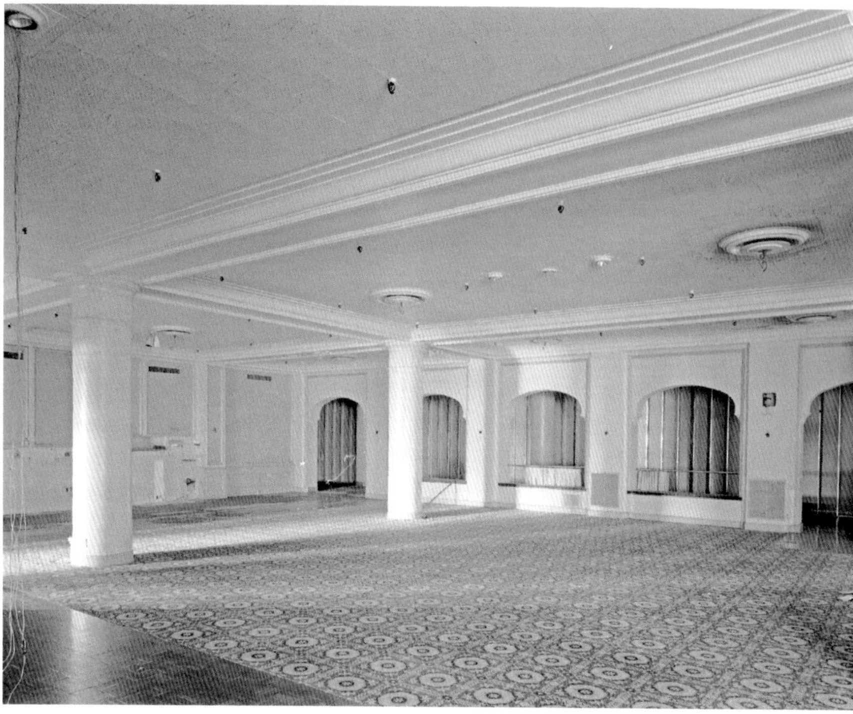

A barren tearoom was a sad sight after its closing in 1990. This was the go-to lunch spot for generations of Indianapolis shoppers. Today, the space is still intact and used for meetings. *Courtesy of the Library of Congress.*

acquired by out-of-state firms. The city was scarred with gaping holes throughout the downtown with the promise of a new shopping mall that many were beginning to doubt would ever come to fruition. This is when the St. Louis–based May and Company announced that the tearoom would be closing by the end of the year. This sparked outrage among the many loyal customers. Letter-writing campaigns were staged, along with protests on Washington Street. Many customers wondered out loud to reporters why a restaurant that was consistently busy would be closed. It turns out, this was only the tip of the iceberg. The folks who flocked to the tearoom apparently were not spending much time on the floors below it. The store was losing money to the tune of $2 to $3 million per year. The closing of the tearoom proved a last-ditch effort to cut costs. One year later, the May Company would shutter the downtown department store and the locally based corporate office. For many, L.S. Ayres existed in name only until it merged with Macy's fifteen years later. Today, the name is completely

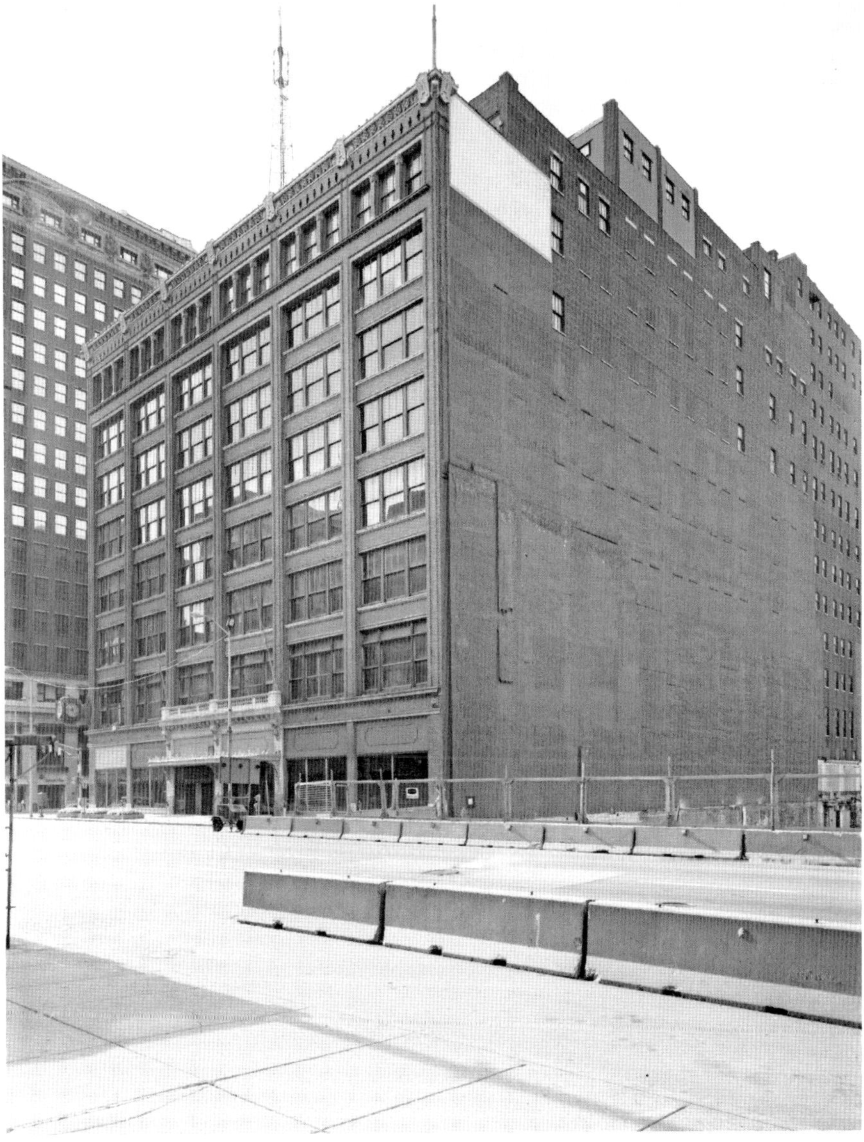

A vacant L.S. Ayres store awaits repurposing on the desolate early 1990s streets of downtown Indianapolis. Notice that you can see the Hyatt Regency in the background, as the entire western portion of this block had been demolished in anticipation of the Circle Centre Mall. *Courtesy of the Library of Congress.*

gone. Thankfully, many of the artifacts were acquired by the Indiana State Museum. A replica tearoom was constructed at the museum; however, it is open only during special occasions. The flagship downtown store now houses a Carson Pierre Scott, along with other businesses. If one feels a little adventurous, she can find the original tearoom still largely intact on the eighth floor.

KEY WEST SHRIMP HOUSE

The drive down south Madison Avenue can be a bit depressing. The once vibrant postwar shopping strip has unfortunately transformed into many discount stores, payday loan outlets and used car dealerships. Shortly after passing Manual High School, one cannot help but be drawn to a structure that appears to be a barnacle-encrusted steamship towering over the surrounding buildings and weed-infested parking lots. It's hard to believe one of the area's top destination restaurants once existed in such an unpleasant environment. This location, however, was where generations of landlocked Hoosiers satisfied cravings for treats from the deep blue sea for over forty years.

The Key West Shrimp House is an iconic name in Indianapolis restaurant lore. Opened in 1950 by Claude Kendall, the restaurant gave area residents a chance to enjoy specialty seafood they would otherwise have to drive hundreds of miles to sample.

The menu indicates that the preferred method of preparation had sea creatures jumping from the deep blue into the deep fryer. As the name suggests, shrimp were in heavy rotation. Guests were treated with complimentary dill pickles, garlic bread and lobster bisque served with each meal. Indiana cities such as Anderson, Bloomington, Madison and Gas City also had locations. Kendall, a tireless promoter, often bought large ads in the paper proclaiming the quality of ingredients and new menu items, ensuring the restaurant was always in forefront of potential diners' consideration.

The restaurant was truly a rarity, lasting for over forty years while providing a high-quality product that customers sought out; however, by 1992, the south side icon found itself at a crossroads. Now being operated by Kendall's daughter, Jackie Mastellone, the time had come to shape up or ship out. Although the restaurant was still busy, the stream of business could no longer support maintaining the massive, aging structure. The roof was in need of replacing, no one could figure out how to paint the building without it peeling in a year's time and the neighborhood was changing. Union Station had become a player in the evolving downtown restaurant scene after reopening as a festival marketplace in 1986. The decision was made to

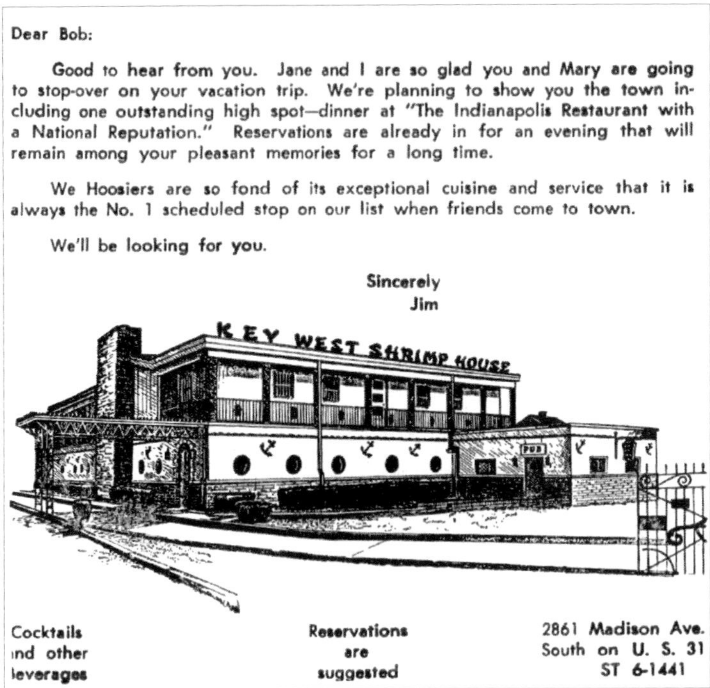

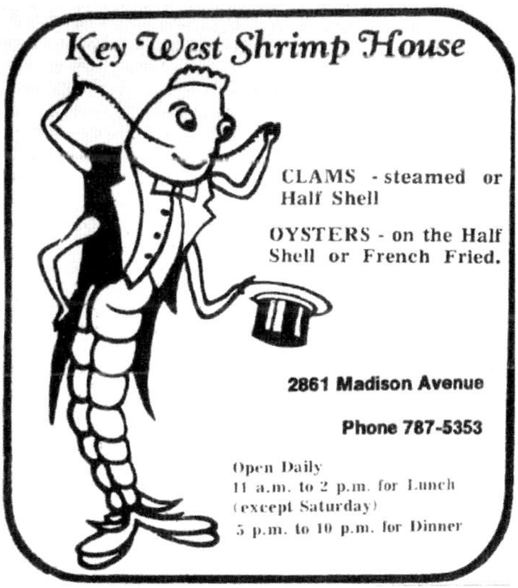

Above: The unique two-story restaurant on Madison Avenue welcomed diners with its nautical theme. The building still stands in a severe state of disrepair, reminding landlocked Hoosiers of what was once an escape to the deep blue sea. *Courtesy of the Indiana State Library.*

Right: An ad depicting a namesake shrimp prior to being coated in coconut and deep fried. *Courtesy of the Indiana State Library.*

move the operation to the heart of the city. The move proved successful, as diners flocked to the new location, yet rough seas were imminent.

The popularity of the "festival marketplace" version of Union Station grew stale in short order. While the quirky shops, massive arcade and

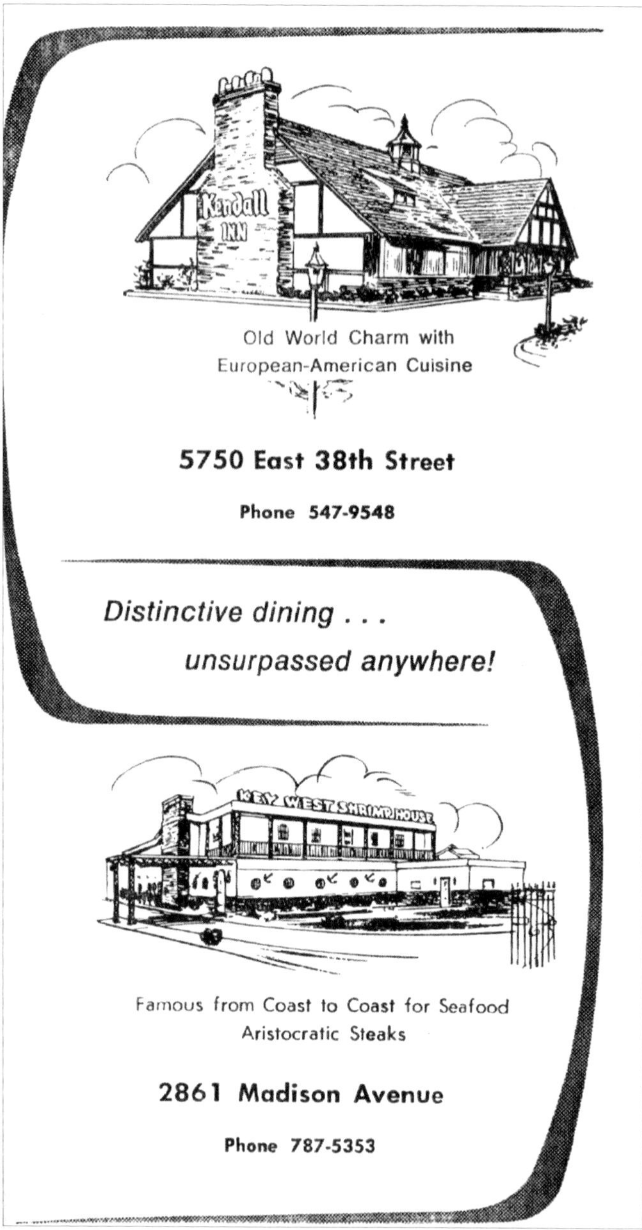

Aside from the Key West Shrimp House, the Kendall family also operated the Kendall Inn on East Thirty-Eighth Street. The restaurant featured musical entertainment and was quite the hotspot in the 1970s. The inn lasted through the mid-'80s but eventually fell victim to the changing economics of the east side. *Courtesy of the Indiana State Library.*

food court were the hub of downtown activity in the late 1980s and early '90s, the opening of the sparkling new Circle Centre Mall in 1995 spelled immediate doom for the station. Customer traffic came to a screeching halt, and most of the stores and restaurants had departed within a year. The Key West Shrimp House managed to stay afloat until 1996 in its new location; however, the city soon closed the landmark to the public. Fortunately, all was not lost. Those craving a seafood fix who are willing to take a road trip can still sample these long-forgotten goodies. The location in Madison, Indiana, on the banks of the Ohio River is still very much open. The restaurant is run by the family of a former Indianapolis manager and appears to provide a similar dining experience. The flagship restaurant still looms large over its surroundings in a serious state of disrepair.

Fireside South

Another Indianapolis south side institution gave credence to this being a "meat and potatoes" type of town—that's the type of reputation one garners from being located some six hundred miles from the nearest coastline. And that's why even today most of the state's popular restaurants tend to be purveyors of USDA prime. The steak market in Indiana has had a number of favorites come and go over the years. One sentimental favorite had the chops to last half a century on Raymond Street.

The name "Fireside" evokes images of a cozy and romantic evening. This is what generations of diners experienced at the restaurant on East Raymond Street, commonly referred to as Fireside South. The restaurant opened in 1946 under the management of brothers Herb and Earnest Hohlt. Steak was the specialty of the house, and many former customers reminisce about the sizzling sound the entrées made as they were carried from the kitchen into the expansive dining room.

Other popular items included prime rib, pork chops and French-fried lobster tail, all served with warm garlic bread. The specialty drink of Fireside was a frozen Brandy Alexander, and anyone wishing to indulge in a nightcap would be sure to order one. Success spelled expansion, and a second "north" location was built at 6440 Westfield Boulevard, near Broad Ripple Village. "Fireside North" lasted only a few years, however; it closed around 1964. The building housed American Legion Post 34 for decades, until 2015, when the property came up for redevelopment.

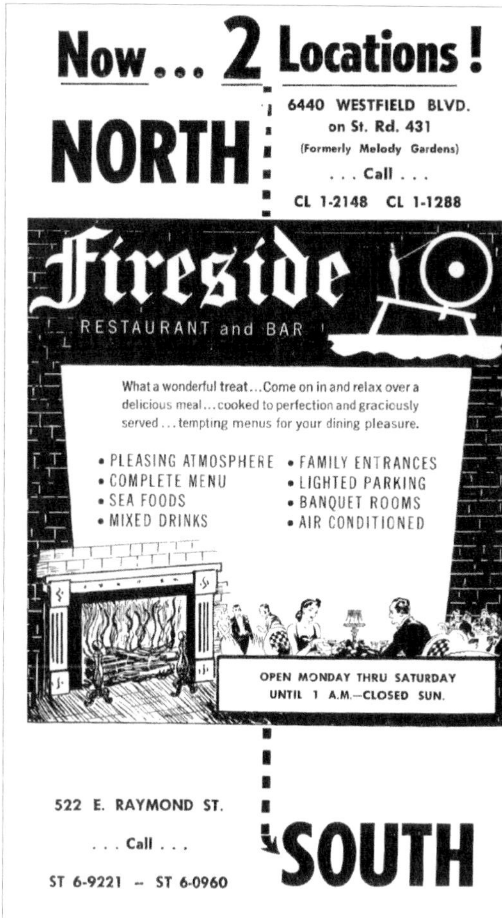

Fireside South was the go-to place for steaks on the south side. The venerable restaurant unfortunately closed in 2006. A location in Broad Ripple didn't prove as popular and lasted only a short time during the early 1960s. *Courtesy of the Indiana State Library.*

The south location remained popular throughout the following decades. In 1985, a brief attempt at "dinner and a helicopter ride" launched at the new Indianapolis Heliport, reportedly featuring the Fireside steaks. By 1989, Herb Hohlt was ready for retirement and turned the reins over to nephew Andy for another long run; however, things were different. Over time, Raymond Street had been widened to the point of abutting the restaurant's doorway, making access difficult. Many customers had also moved farther away from the inner-city steakhouse. This, coupled with its residential location with few other entertainment options, spelled the end of Fireside in 2001.

Closing aside, the Hohlt family didn't stay out of the restaurant business for long. In 2009, Andy opened Sammy's Pizza in Greenwood, keeping alive their tradition of a family-run restaurant on the south side. The former restaurant location on Raymond Street has recently housed an art supply house and an empanada business but remained vacant in 2015.

Chapter 3

CRUISING DOWN NORTH MERIDIAN

We've all heard the old cliché "all that glitters is not gold." The saying could definitely apply to what was known as "the strip" in Indianapolis. When today's citizens hear about "the strip," their minds immediately go to the block of rowdy bars geared toward college-aged kids in Broad Ripple Village. That would not have been the case fifty years ago.

Beginning in the early 1950s, Indianapolis's chief entertainment district centered on north Meridian Street, beginning around Twelfth Street and stretching all the way up past Fall Creek. In the early days, this was the place to go for Las Vegas–style entertainment. Posh nightclubs were either erected or moved into stately Victorian-era mansions. Most provided lavish dinners, along with entertainment that ranged from piano music all the way to the A-list performers of the day. While the lavish experience was enjoyed by many, it often covered up a sinister back story. Often, these businesses served as fronts for owners involved in organized crime and the vices associated with it. By the 1960s, the "sin strip" had become the target of vice raids put on by grandstanding politicians and prosecutors. At the same time, the surrounding neighborhoods were in severe decline, and the area was perceived as dangerous. The once posh supper clubs slowly went away and were replaced by clubs that catered to a much different crowd. One by one, these establishments began to disappear as extreme poverty took hold of the neighborhood streets to the east and west and Interstate 65 cut the area off from downtown. By 1977, only two lounges remained. The final holdout, Shannon's Roaring Twenties, whimpered out after a police raid in May

1997, marking the end of "the strip." The next few pages will focus on some of the older establishments that managed to stay on the right side of the thin blue line and public perception.

The Hawthorn Room

Where cars now fight for a position in the McDonald's drive-through, there once was one of the truly good places to eat in midtown. The Hawthorn Room was a fixture at Sixteenth and Meridian for over thirty years. The Hawthorn Room began serving in 1942. The pretty white building featured a covered porte-cochère and expansive bay windows for diners to view the bustling traffic. The main dining room was centered on a large apple tree.

The restaurant was started by the owners of the Seville, located downtown. It was strictly nonalcoholic, however, and thus became a staple for many sorority meetings and other women's clubs. The longevity of the staff and consistent quality helped establish a long list of regular customers. Chef Cleo Edwards oversaw the kitchen for nearly the entire life of the restaurant. He prided himself on made-from-scratch home cooking. Some signature menu items included a succulent roto-steak, pressure-fried chicken and the Hawthorn's trademark butterscotch rolls. Diners had little chance of ever leaving hungry, as the restaurant included an appetizer, salad, two side dishes and dessert with every meal.

Over time, the restaurant was expanded, adding the garden room in the area where the driveway once protruded. Soon, the restaurant overtook the house to the north, adding the saddle room and the 500 room, which featured a hand-painted mural of the start of the legendary race in May.

Things were not meant to last, however. The restaurant closed in 1974 after a change in ownership the previous year. Three years later, a local franchisee built a McDonald's on the former site of the Hawthorn Room. McDonald's is still serving its billions, albeit in a different building. The days of leisurely meals at one of the city's busiest corners are now a distant memory.

Martinique Lounge

Just down from the Hawthorn Restaurant was a bit of a different establishment. The Martinique Lounge can trace its roots all the way back to 1873. That's when the massive Italianate house at number 946 was constructed. Although hard to fathom today, North Meridian Street was a purely residential boulevard prior to the beginning of the twentieth century. Stately private residences would have been considered commonplace. The home served various private residences up until 1900. At this point, it was expanded upward and began serving as an exclusive hotel. Sometime in the early 1940s, a final metamorphosis occurred that converted the home into twenty apartments. Those apartment dwellers would not have peace and quiet for long. In 1950, the Martinique Lounge opened. Taking a page from the French colony in the Caribbean, the Martinique took on a pirate theme. The lounge boasted nightly entertainment and "fine foods."

The nightclub actually closed in 1962 for a couple years but got a second chance in life. This time around, the focus was strictly on the food. New owner Jack Ensly dubbed the Martinique "the most romantic restaurant in town." Under Ensly's leadership, the restaurant was redecorated to reflect his desire to provide Indianapolis with a fine restaurant in the French manner. Some house specialties included beef tenderloin tips en casserole, chicken pot pie, seafood selections and prime rib. The revival was short-lived, however. During the mid-1960s, organized crime was taking hold of many near north side nightclubs and using intimidation to squelch the competition. In December 1964, a suspicious fire was set in the kitchen. Although the Martinique did briefly reopen, it would close forever in 1965. By 1968, the B.F. Goodrich tire company had purchased the property where the elegant old house sat. The Martinique was demolished, and a new tire showroom was erected. So much for progress!

The Keys

Another converted house on north Meridian Street served as what was possibly the swankiest of the north side supper clubs. The mansion, located in the 1800 block, was constructed around 1890. For many years, the house was home to the Gates family, proprietors of the lavish Severin Hotel.

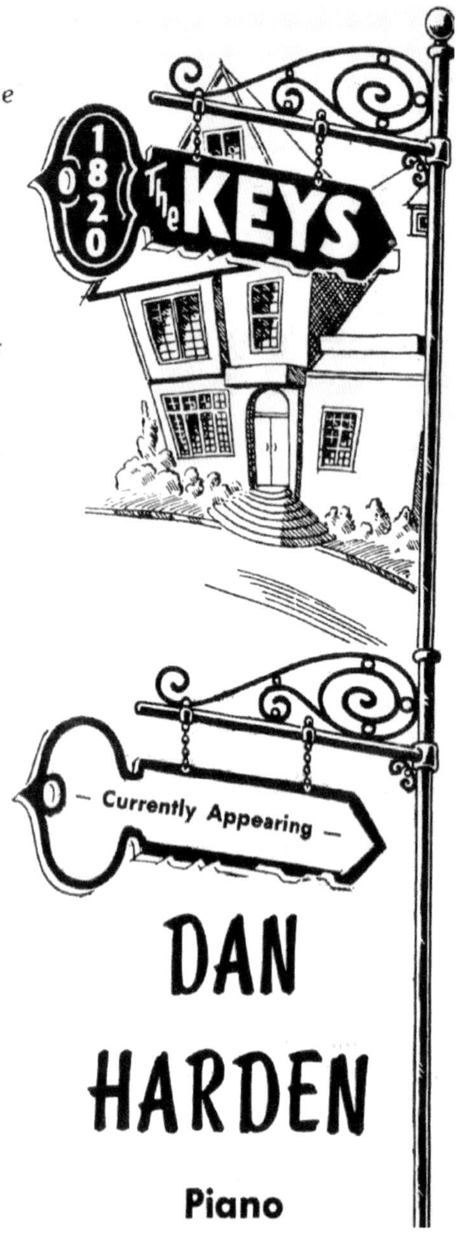

The Keys was famous for its world-class food and upstairs piano lounge. The piano lounge was later converted into a private dining room featuring rare works of art. *Courtesy Indiana State Library.*

In 1947, the home was converted into The Keys restaurant. The lower floor was made into the main dining room and cocktail lounge. The upstairs portion of the house boasted the first piano bar in Indiana. The establishment, owned by Mary Helen Krafft, quickly garnered a reputation for outstanding food. In 1957, The Keys won *Holiday* magazine's annual restaurant award and would hold on to it for an unprecedented nine consecutive years.

The tradition of excellence would unfortunately end. In 1970, Mary's husband, Bill, sold the Monarch Buick dealership he owned on Meridian Street, and the couple drifted into retirement. By 1973, The Keys had been silenced, and a new restaurant, Le Chalet, took up residence in the stately home. The building that once hosted many special occasions and celebrities was demolished in the mid-1980s.

The Embers

Many establishments featured elegantly appointed cocktail lounges and dining rooms and live entertainment. One of the most prominent of these venues was The Embers, located at 2034 North Meridian Street. The entertainment mecca was started in 1960 by businessman William Ball. Ball held partial ownership in the Haag drugstore chain and Huddle Restaurants. According to a 1960s promotional postcard:

> *Ablaze with fiery color, the Embers Cocktail Lounge is a welcome oasis at the end of a tiring day. The finest beverages, prepared by knowing hands, quench the thirst and sharpen the appetite. Through the wall at the left, separating the cocktail lounge from the Embers dining room, guests can see and hear some of the country's finest entertainers who are featured nightly.*

The cocktail lounge provided a dimly lit oasis for the downtown officeworkers of the time. Chairs were upholstered in leather and arranged around small, round tables. Each table was appointed with a large crystal ashtray so one could enjoy his Lucky Strike with his Tom Collins:

> *A pattern of chariot wheels in sculptured concrete accents the individual charm of this delightful dining room. Flaming swords and a blazing charcoal pit make dinner at The Embers a memorable and exciting experience. On the stage at the left, the country's finest entertainers provide a refreshing escape from the day's routine.*

The subtle lounge was coupled with an extravagant main dining room. Tables were adorned with white table cloths and elaborate place settings. A charcoal barbecue was in full display for the patrons, so they could ensure firsthand that their chop didn't get overdone. Entertainment from national touring acts—from the likes of John Coltrane to the Amazing Kreskin—was featured nightly

The shelf life of a hotspot is not always long. The World War II generation that would have frequented The Embers gave way to the baby boomers, who considered such an atmosphere stuffy and contrived. In a candid interview, owner William Ball gave a much different account upon the closure of his nightclub in 1970. He credited the closure to be the result of crime going on unchecked. He painted a picture of drug addicts and ladies of the evening harassing the few customers who still bothered to venture into the neighborhood. The once posh nightclubs that lined Meridian Street from Sixteenth to Fall Creek devolved, eventually catering to a seedier crowd as the 1960s became the '70s. The site now boasts a large surface parking lot for Citizens Energy employees.

La Rue's Supper Club

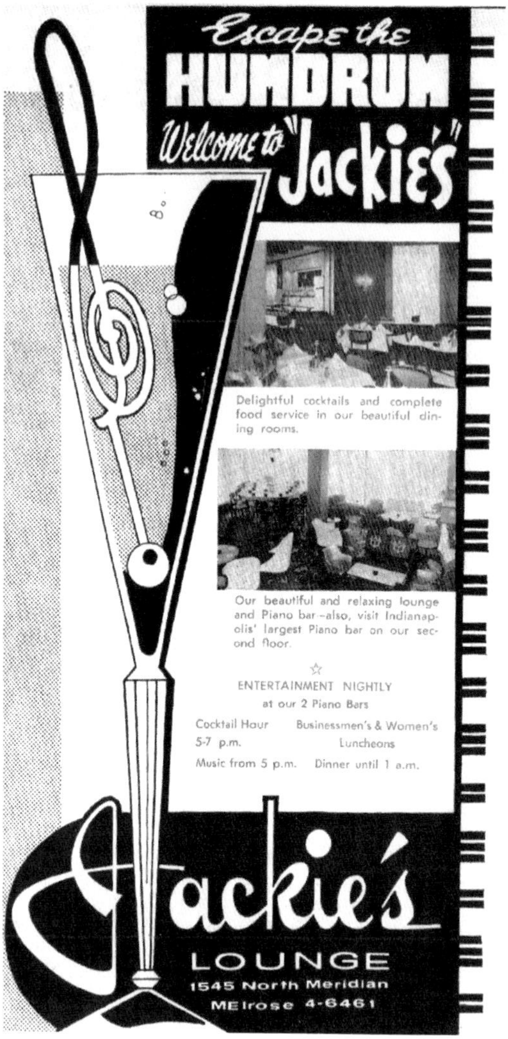

Jackie's on North Meridian Street was one of the longest-running establishments on the city's "sin strip," lasting from 1956 until the late '70s. *Courtesy of the Indiana State Library.*

In 1871, a famous name in Indianapolis constructed a mansion at 1121 North Pennsylvania Street. Albert Fletcher, the youngest son of city father Calvin Fletcher, spared no cost in constructing the home. Woodwork was imported from southern France and northern Italy. Around the turn of the century, the Clune family occupied the home, installing electricity. The house served as a private residence until 1930, when it was converted to office space.

In 1946, the grand old house was converted into La Rue's Supper Club, providing lunch, dinner and assorted music each day until 12:30 a.m. Owner Harley Horton got the idea to open the club so that regular people could have a nice place to go without having to join an expensive country club. The first floor of the building featured the "gold room," an elaborately decorated dining area. The specialty of the house was a plank steak, a steak served on a wooden plank surrounded by seasoned whipped potatoes. The second floor was a posh club area that served as the first home to the Antelope Club, which remains in existence today, albeit in a different location. The club

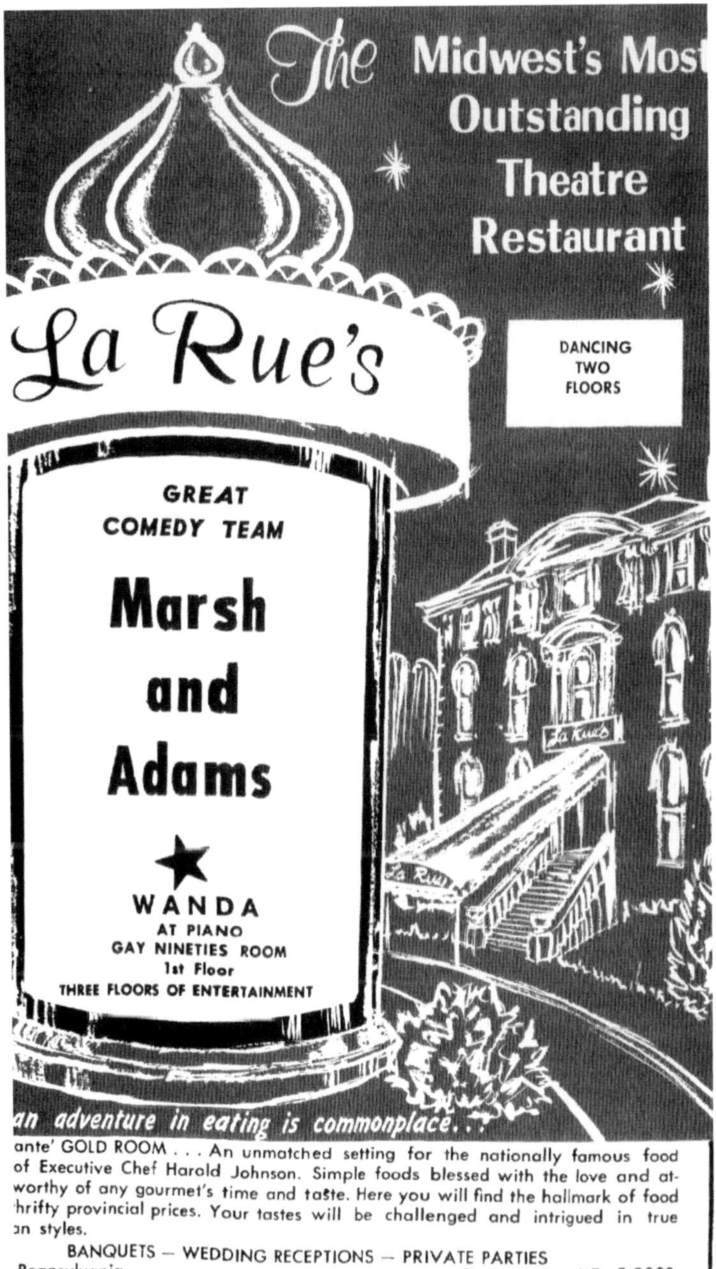

La Rue's was one of the first postwar nightclubs in Indianapolis. The club was located just east of Meridian on Pennsylvania Street in the historic Albert Fletcher mansion. The club operated into the late 1960s, but the historic house eventually succumbed to Interstate 65. *Courtesy of the Indiana State Library.*

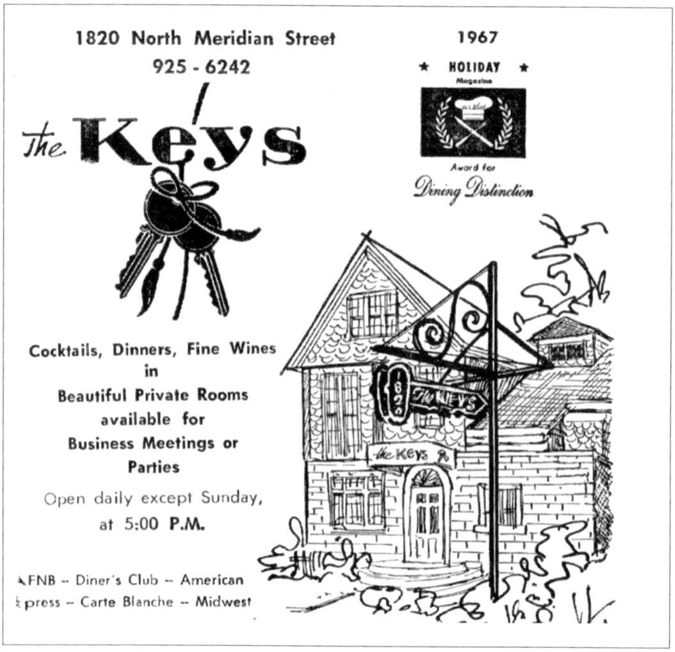

The Keys was noted for its nightly piano entertainment. The old Victorian home that housed the restaurant and nightclub is long gone, and the place where it once stood is now surrounded by office buildings. *Courtesy of the Indiana State Library.*

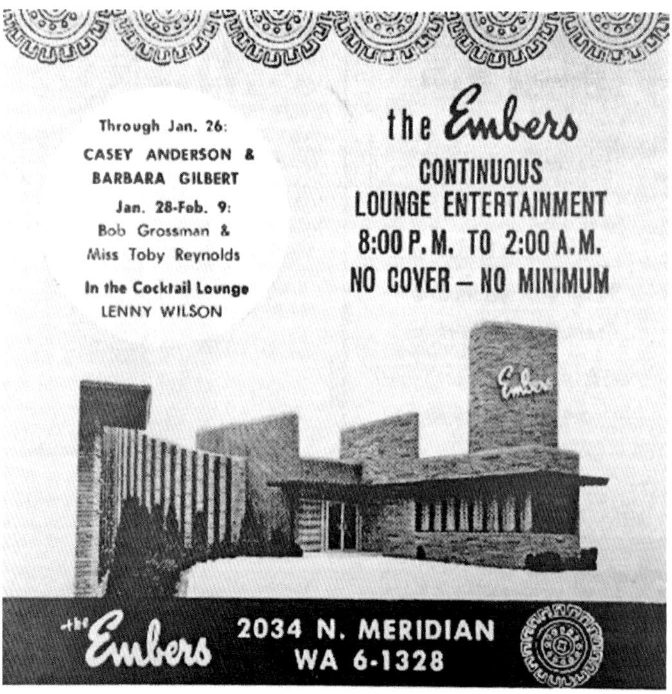

This ad for The Embers shows off its swanky, modern building. As the Meridian Street strip devolved in the late 1960s, a high-class entertainment venue no longer served the needs of customers. The Embers had closed by 1971. *Courtesy of the Indiana State Library.*

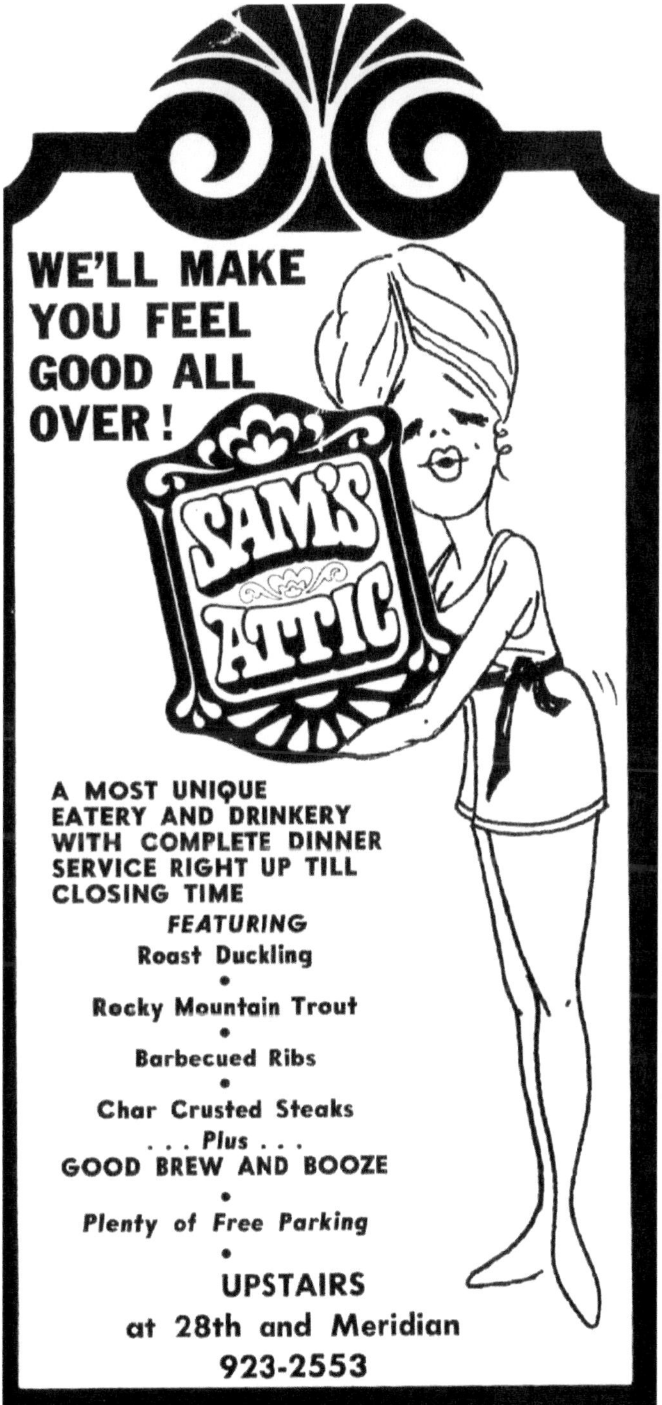

Sam's Attic sat above the flagship Sam's Subway and was the nightlife offering of the restaurant group's portfolio. The lounge featured a relaxed atmosphere and "off-color" drink names. *Courtesy of the Indiana State Library.*

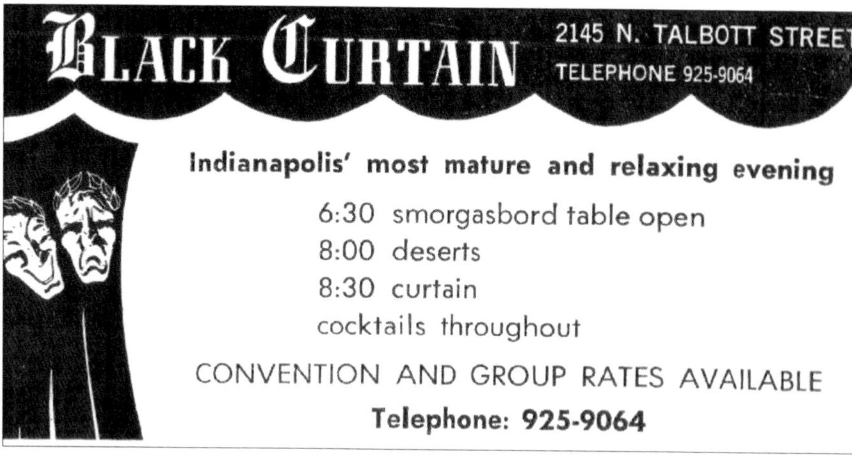

Set up in an old movie house, the Black Curtain offered musical entertainment. The dinner theater anchored a Bohemian area of the city known as Talbott Village. This served as an upper-class destination in an otherwise deteriorating environment. The theater lasted from 1968 until 1980. Today, a nightclub occupies the spot in a rapidly redeveloping neighborhood. *Courtesy of the Indiana State Library.*

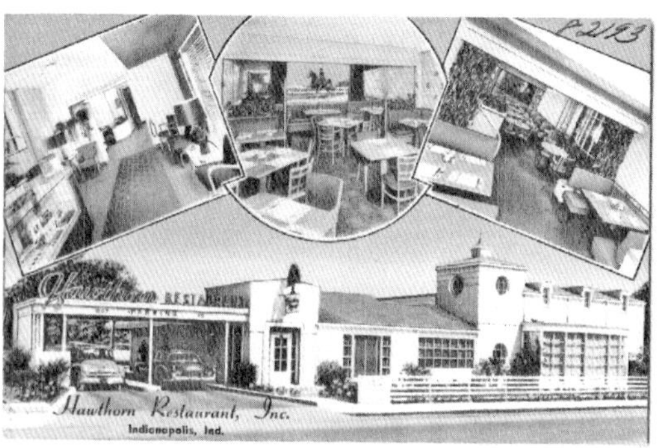

The Hawthorn Restaurant was long known as a good dining destination, especially for the lunch crowd. The restaurant began serving up hungry diners in 1944 and lasted through 1974. Today, the site is a McDonald's restaurant. *Courtesy of the Boston Public Library.*

prospered throughout the 1950s despite run-ins with the city liquor board concerning the multiple businesses Horton ran from the club.

By the mid-1960s, La Rue's was facing a dwindling clientele and was forced into bankruptcy in 1965. The grand house unfortunately would not hold on for much longer. After being acquired by the state highway department, the structure met the wrecking ball in 1967. Today, there is no trace of the posh destination, as it is buried under the concrete of Interstate 65.

Sam's Subway Restaurant Group

Many lifelong Indianapolis residents continue to reminisce about a group of restaurants that made a pretty good run at being everything to everyone. The Sam's Restaurant Group operated locations all across town, offering deli lunches, lavish dinners and swanky nightlife. Known for their high-quality food preparations and wild themes, nothing really exists today that can compare to the experiences the Hochman family delivered for over fifty years.

In 1907, a young man by the name of Sam Hochman arrived in Indianapolis from New York City and would change the way the city thought of theme dining. He started his first restaurant on College Avenue near Eighteenth Street. Ten years later, he made a big splash. Sam's Subway opened in 1928 "where Meridian crosses 28th." The restaurant took the "subway" name, as it was located in the lower level of an apartment building. This was a full-service restaurant that also featured a delicatessen serving up kosher products. Popular items included steaks, kabobs, shrimp cocktails and Rueben sandwiches. The restaurant proved a hit and gradually expanded to include four dining rooms.

Things really took off when Sam's sons, Harry and Saul, joined after World War II. The group had the foresight to recognize changing population patterns and quickly opened outposts at the new suburban shopping centers. Glendale Center and Eastgate had their own versions of the popular downtown location, while a themed Crown Room opened in the Meadows. The Crown Room focused heavily on entertainment and featured national touring acts. Soon, they had an empire of around a dozen restaurants scattered throughout the city. The Meridian Street location definitely didn't suffer because of the growth. Throughout the 1950s and '60s, the flagship Sam's would be in a state of near constant expansion and remodeling. There was The Attic, which served as a late night cocktail lounge, complete with risqué cocktail names such as the "Slow Screw." Sam's Bedroom featured booths designed to look like beds. The addition of Sam's Basement completed the happy house.

In May 1973, a wild new concept from the Sam's Restaurant group was unearthed. The Caves and Caverns took theme dining to the next level. The dining room was built out to resemble a subterranean cavern, complete with stalactites and stalagmites. "Cave pits" could host groups of up to ten and were situated along a winding path. Everything was covered in decorative concrete. Advertising copy from the 1970s reaffirms the playful nature of Sam's:

Relax baby and wear whatever turns you on because the Caves 'n Cavern is having an Un-Party! No set time, no set menu...no special decorations. Just eat what you want, drink what you want and be with your friends... or make some new ones! Come on in, unwind and lose yourself in the unique atmosphere of the "Caves." The unusual décor of the "Caves" is constructed of cement and is therefore fireproof!

Unfortunately, by the mid-1970s, the business climate had begun to change for Sam's Restaurant Group. Locations at Eastgate and the Meadows suffered from a rapidly changing business environment as the once popular shopping centers declined.

The worst blow came in April 1978, when the legendary Sam's Subway at Twenty-Eighth and Meridian Streets closed forever after fifty years in business. The remaining restaurants at Glendale, the Indiana State Teachers Association Building and the Caves and Caverns remained open for a while; however, overexpansion crippled the struggling company with debt.

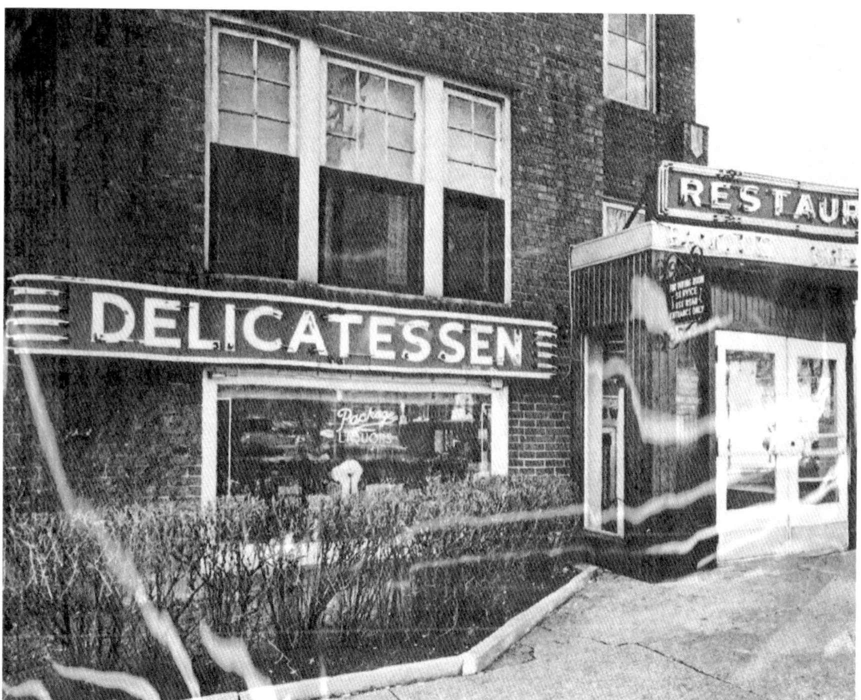

The exterior of Sam's Subway. The legendary restaurant was famous for its great food and ever-evolving themes. *Courtesy of Faith Cohen.*

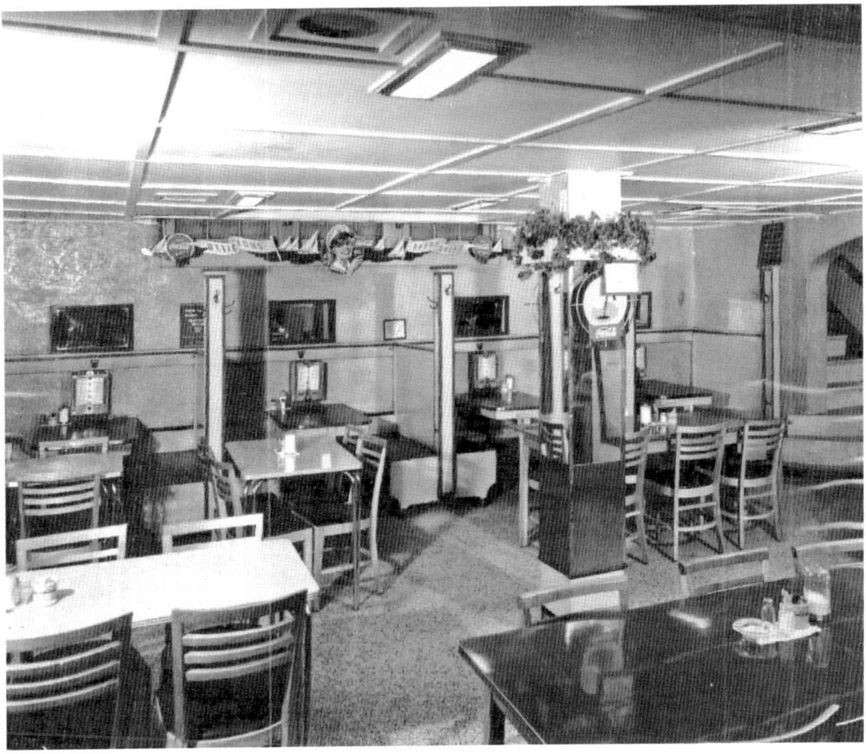

Above: The interior of Sam's Subway features an Art Deco look in this photograph. The subterranean location is the reasoning behind the name. *Courtesy of Faith Cohen.*

Right: Sam Hochman and sons, Harry and Saul, ruled over Sam's restaurant empire. *Courtesy of Faith Cohen.*

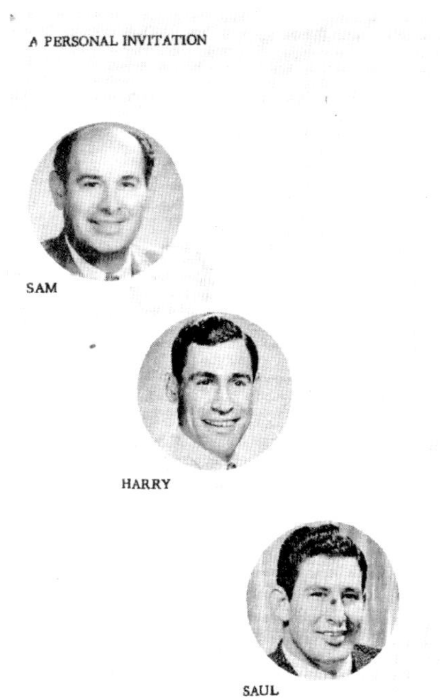

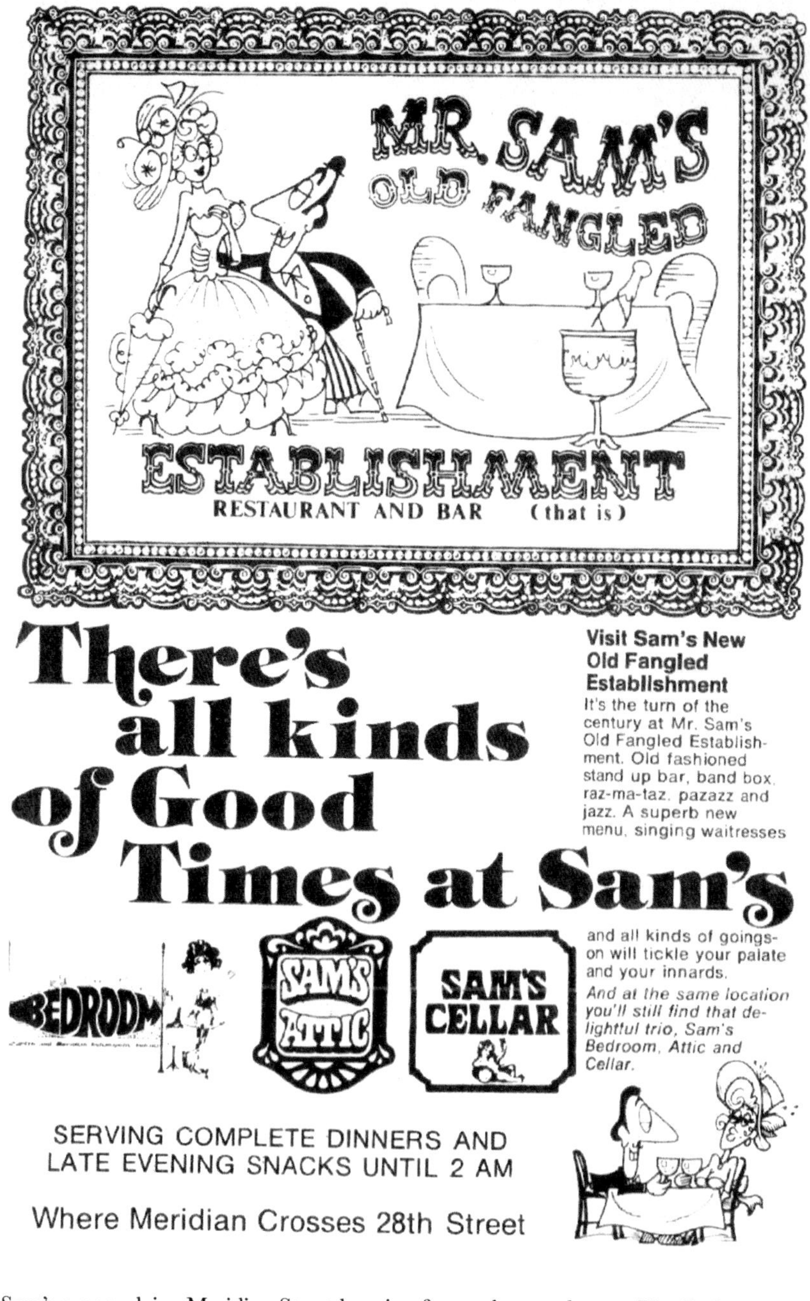

Sam's ever-evolving Meridian Street location featured many themes. The Bedroom actually featured seating designed to look like beds. Late hours were kept to harness business from the night owls who roamed Meridian Street in mid-century Indianapolis. *Courtesy of the Indiana State Library.*

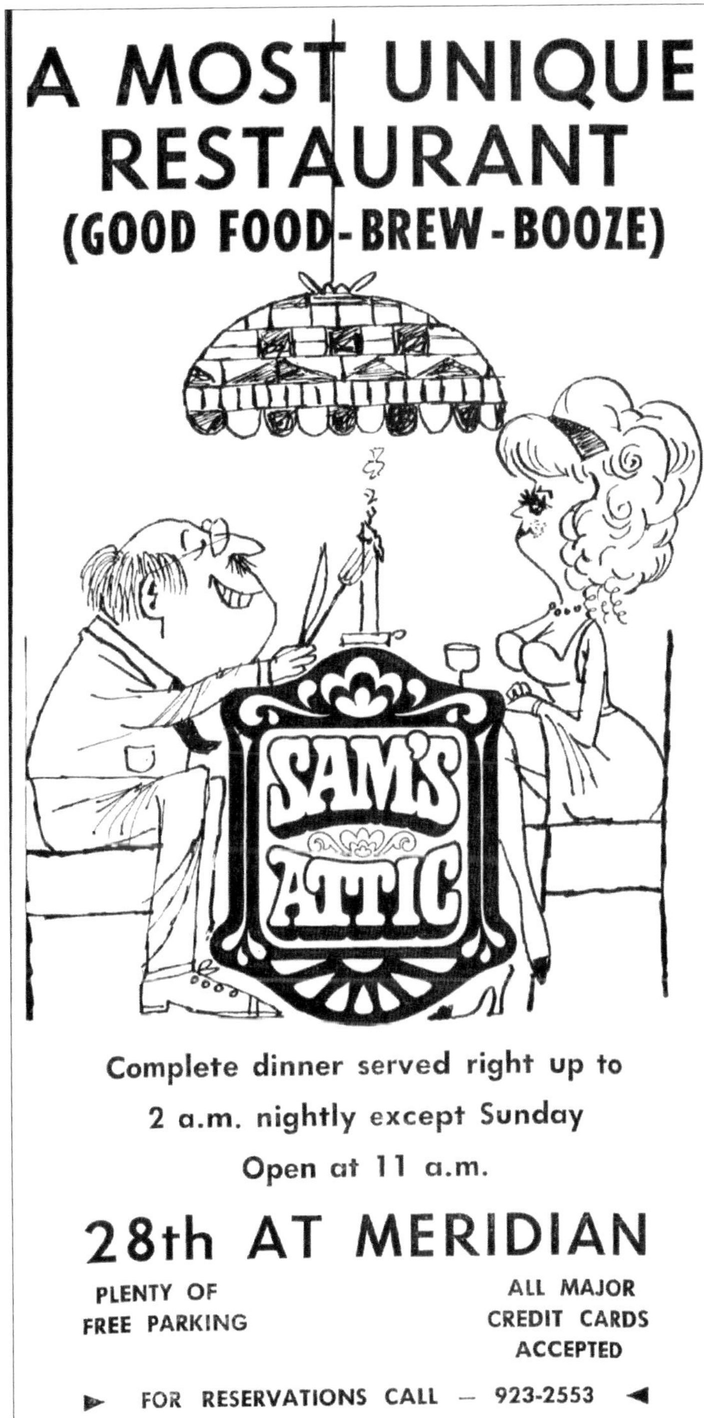

Another ad for the myriad restaurants located at Sam's on north Meridian Street. The legendary location closed in 1977. *Courtesy of the Indiana State Library.*

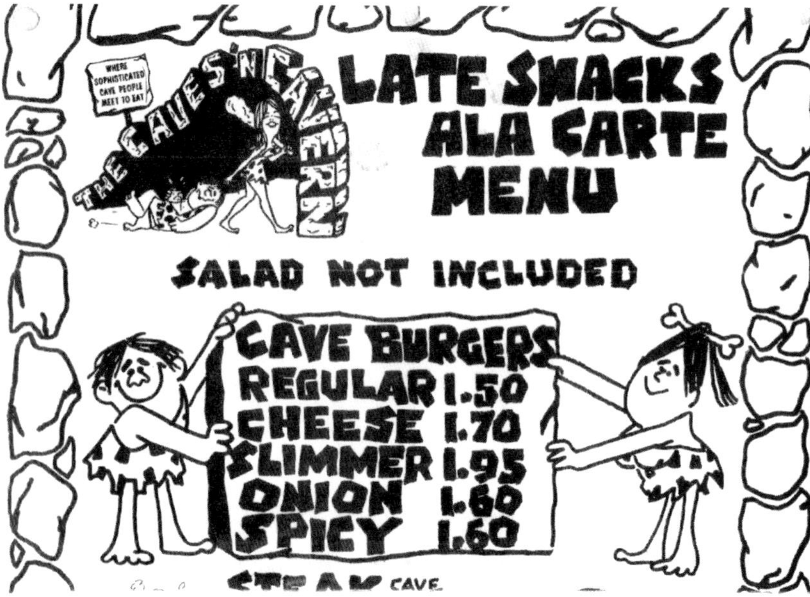

One of the later concepts Sam's Restaurant Group tried was called the Caves and Caverns. The restaurant, located on Eighty-Sixth Street across from North Central High School, was decorated as a cave. Diners sat on rock formations amid the stalactites and stalagmites. *Courtesy of Faith Cohen.*

The venerable Glendale Center saw the last Sam's Subway close in 1981. Meanwhile, North Meridian Street had essentially hit rock bottom. The Lilly Endowment stepped up in 1982 to help clean up the blight. It purchased several abandoned buildings along Meridian Street, including the restaurant Sam Cohen had opened nearly sixty years earlier, and unceremoniously tore them down.

Faith Cohen, daughter of the late Harry Hochman, still resides on the north side of Indianapolis. She is proud of the legacy the Sam's Restaurant Group built over the half century it fed the people of Indianapolis. During the turbulent civil rights era of the 1950s and '60s, Sam's restaurants were open to all races as both a place to eat and a place of employment. The commitment to quality food never wavered. All menu items were house made, including the breads and pastries. Today, Cohen maintains a Facebook page where former customers and employees can reminisce about this beloved, uniquely Indiana institution.

Chapter 4

INTERNATIONAL FLAIR

The "Did you Notice" column in the *Indianapolis News* on October 2, 1967, noted "the bearded man looking every bit like a maharaja looking over an art display at 7:30 a.m., today, in the City-County lobby." This was in reference to K.P. Singh, an Indian immigrant and member of Sikh faith, shortly after he moved to Indiana. You see, the Indianapolis population at the time primarily consisted of Western European immigrants and African Americans and would remain that way through the 1980s. Rarely did anyone encounter emigrants from Latin America, Africa, Asia or Eastern Europe. This is why K.P. Singh stood out enough for the local media to take notice half a century ago. Things are much different today.

Singh took this opportunity to educate the population and become a leader in cultural and civic matters. You can see his artwork displayed at many places across the city. Today, the international population of Indianapolis is growing and flourishing. What was once thought of as a homogenous midwestern state capital now boasts nearly 100,000 of its citizenry hailing from a foreign country. Nearly 10 percent alone have come from a Latin American country. Recent years also brought a large Burmese refugee population settling in the south side of the city. Not only have refugees seeking a better life flocked to the Circle City, but also many large employers have relocated international employees to work in highly skilled positions. This has resulted in a dramatic change in our food culture. The long-forgotten retail corridor situated around the Lafayette Square Mall has transformed into an international marketplace. Here, one can find restaurants from all corners of the earth. International groceries and marketplaces are numerous as first-generation immigrants strive to preserve important cultural traditions in their new home.

The population demographics that K.P. Singh faced back in 1967 stood at 81.6 percent white (non-Hispanic) and 18.0 percent African American, according to the U.S. Census Bureau. Despite this complete lack of diversity, there were several pioneering families who opened ethnic restaurants across the city, sharing their cultures with the meat and potato–loving Hoosiers.

Italian! Italian!

One of the largest early immigrant populations in Indianapolis were the Italians. The population had exploded to over one thousand by the turn of the century, and these immigrants dominated the food industry and the arts. By 1910, thirty-three of thirty-four produce dealers were Italian. Artisans decorated churches and private homes with paintings, along with terrazzo and marble flooring. Many Italian immigrants settled on the near southeast side of downtown, in the Fletcher Place neighborhood, creating one of the first ethnic enclaves. Today, this area retains many clues to its ethnic past. The Ray and Mascari tomato-packing plant is located on South Street. Farther east, along South College Avenue, two legacy Italian restaurants stand nearly side by side. The Italian Street Festival held each June by the Holy Rosary Catholic Church is also widely popular.

Iaria's Italian Restaurant

For years, Indianapolis residents have flocked to an unassuming buff-colored building on the near southeast side. Once inside the decisively old-school building, diners are treated to some of the best Italian food in the city. Iaria's has been a staple in the city for over a century now. Menu favorites include spaghetti with giant meatballs, thin-crust pizzas loaded with homemade sausage and lasagna. All come with Iaria's signature red sauce.

In 1905, an Italian immigrant from Roccaforte came to the United States with the prospects of working in a coal mine in West Virginia. After five years of toiling away in the notoriously bad conditions, in 1910, Peter Iaria escaped to Indianapolis, where he opened a stand in the city market. In the midst of the Great Depression, Iaria constructed his namesake tavern and bowling alley at 317 South Noble Street (now College Avenue) in 1935. He would run his namesake business until 1942, when he turned it over to his son Peter Jr. Despite negative attention from the state liquor commission and neighbors, the tavern thrived. Ten years later, the establishment closed up shop; however, this was hardly goodbye. The wooden-frame building was demolished, and a brand-new structure rose from the site, boasting air conditioning and an adjacent bowling alley. Advertisements of the time promised spaghetti dinners in ultra-modern surroundings. The restaurant thrived over the next three decades and became popular with visiting celebrities and race car drivers, who came for the pizzas and succulent red sauce served with the many pasta dishes. It seemed like the good times would go on forever.

But things don't always run smoothly in a family business. In 2001, a well-publicized feud erupted after a plot to short-sell the restaurant was discovered by other family members. Iaria's closed its doors in July just before the Brickyard 400. Cooler heads eventually prevailed, and the restaurant reopened a few days later. Iaria's was threatened again in 2003, when matriarch Kathleen Iaria fell ill. After sitting dormant for nearly two months, a group of nieces and nephews of majority owner Nick Iaria teamed

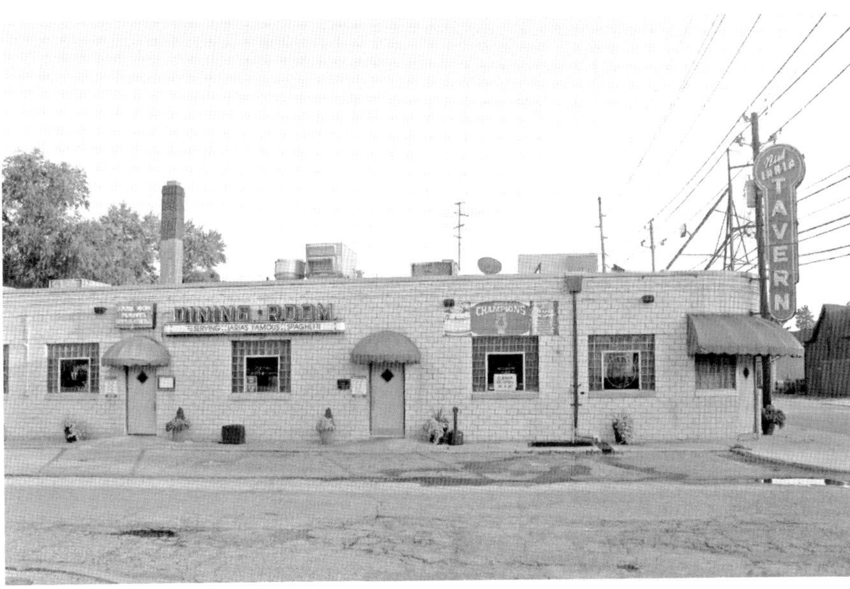

Iaria's has been serving up classic Italian fare since 1913. The southeast side landmark has an old-school vibe and is a local favorite. *Courtesy of Jeff Kamm.*

up to purchase the family namesake. The restaurant reopened in October 2003, although without the adjacent bowling alley. The restaurant continues to provide the same great experience to this day.

Macri's Italian Village

Looking for a spot to have a nice romantic dinner? Few things set the mood more than a candle-lit dinner at an Italian restaurant, and Indianapolis has been blessed with a fine selection of locally based purveyors of pasta. Looking back on one particular institution that lasted for over forty years, you could say that it was known just as much for its colorful owner as it was for its food.

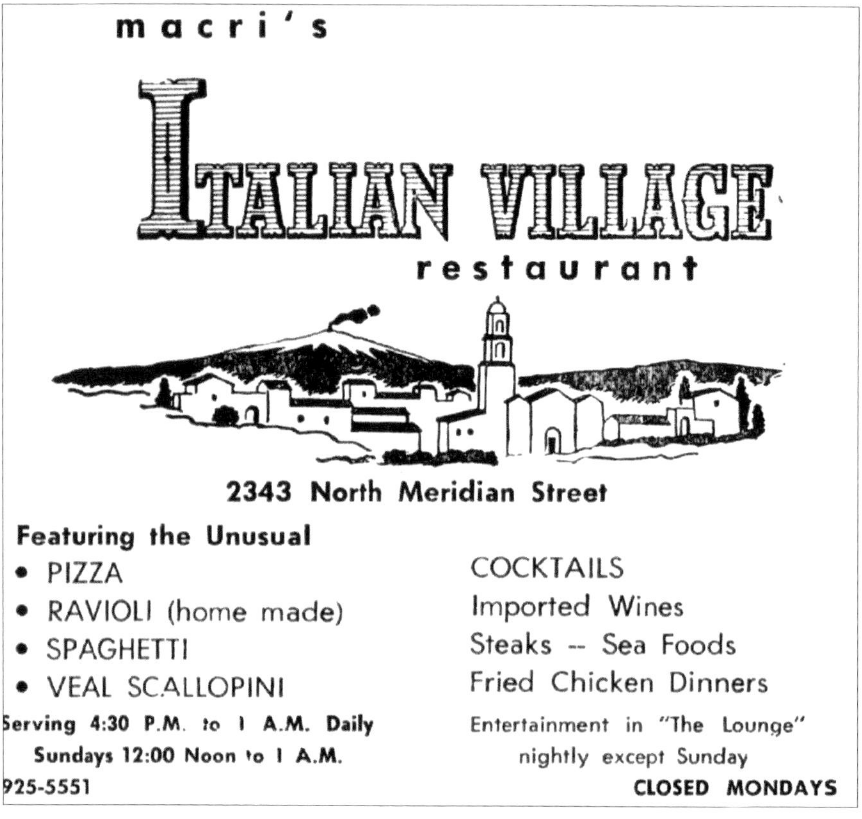

Macri's Italian Village is yet another one of the lost destinations that lined North Meridian Street in the 1950s and '60s. The restaurant ended up relocating to a motel in suburban Carmel until its closing in the 1990s. *Courtesy of the Indiana State Library.*

Macri's Italian Village opened in 1951 at 2343 North Meridian Street in a former residence. This was prime real estate on which much of the postwar social life in Indianapolis was centered. The Italian Village was surrounded by numerous swanky nightclubs and other high-end dining options. Known for a spectacular antipasti buffet, another item regular diners seemed to rave about were the unique deep-fried carrots.

A key to any restaurant's success is consistency, not only in food, but in management as well. The Italian Village was owned throughout nearly its entire run by World War II veteran Silvo "John" Macri. Surprisingly enough, the restaurant business would not be Mr. Macri's sole passion. He was a nationally known numerologist. Numerology is the belief that there is a divine relationship between numbers and corresponding events. Numerologists serve as sort of mathematical fortunetellers. Mr. Macri gave hundreds of lectures across the country and later served as personal consultant to celebrities such as Liberace, the Amazing Kreskin and Rita Moreno.

The restaurant was always successful, despite going through several locations. When the decline of North Meridian became too much to bear in the 1970s, the Italian Village moved to the shopping center at Keystone and Fifty-Second Streets. This incarnation of the Italian Village lasted until 1978. The final location, through the mid-1990s, was the much-maligned Carmel Motel, which stood at U.S. Highway 31 and Old Meridian Street, well north of Indianapolis. Mr. Macri passed away in March 1996, after retiring two years earlier. Shortly thereafter, the restaurant closed, as the motel gained more attention from Carmel leaders and the local media for being a magnet for clientele not typically associated with the posh suburb. The entire complex is long gone, along with the original location of the restaurant on Meridian Street.

Milano Inn

Everyone loves a happy ending. When owners of locally owned restaurants face retirement, the futures of these beloved spots can become a bit murky. Such was the case in the late 1970s with a popular Italian restaurant, the Milano Inn. Thankfully, through the hard work of new owners, the southeast side landmark exists today bigger and better than ever.

In 1934, a building located in the Fletcher Place neighborhood was converted from a pool hall into one of the most enduring family-owned Italian eateries in the city. The restaurant was the dream of Joe and Mari

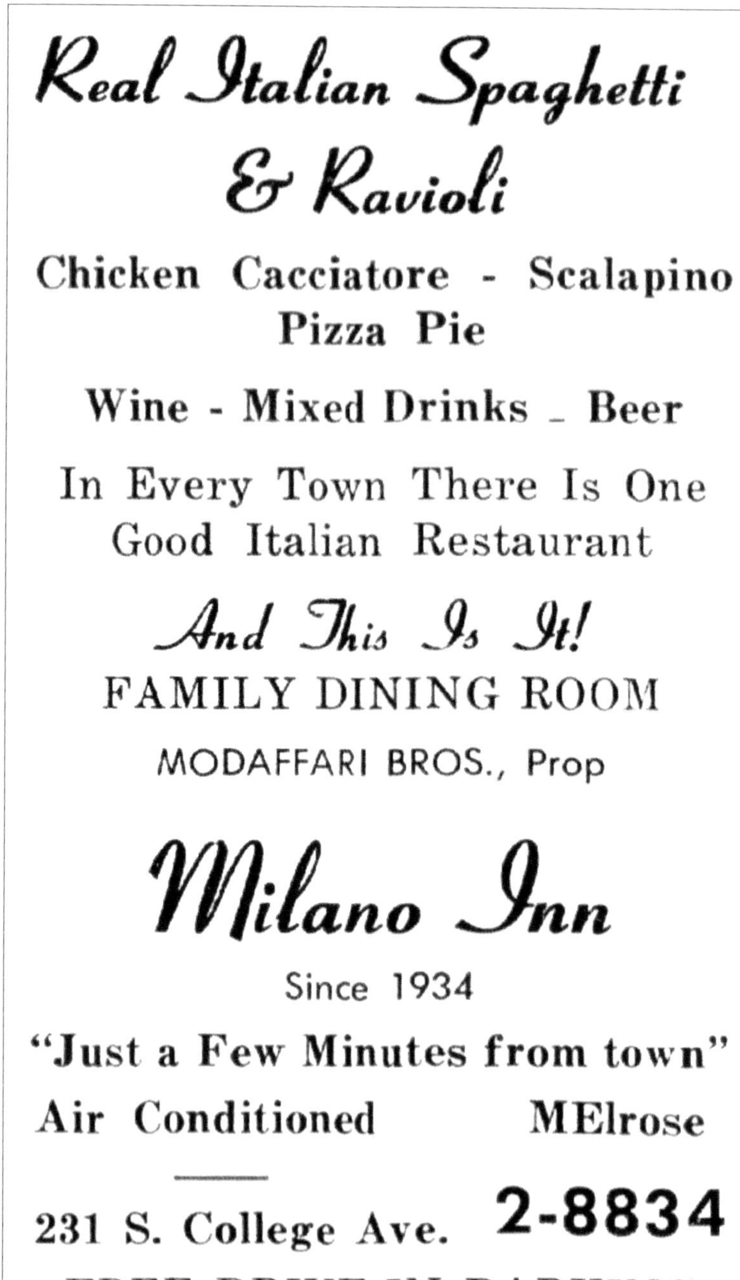

The Milano Inn remains an institution, having been located on South College Avenue since the Depression. *Courtesy of the Indiana State Library.*

Modaffari. Mr. Modaffari was an immigrant from Roccaforte, Italy. He arrived in the United States with his brother Paul in 1907. The brothers started in the burgeoning south side produce business until Uncle Sam came calling for World War I. Upon the brothers' successful return from the war, they started the Milano Inn. The duo ran a popular restaurant throughout the next two decades. Unfortunately, they would be sidelined with illness, with Joe passing away in 1961 and Paul in 1964. The popular restaurant then came under the control of Paul's widow, Mary, through the rest of the 1960s, until she sold it in 1970. After her "retirement," Mary continued to work part time in the dining room.

The restaurant limped on through the 1970s as various family members attempted to keep things afloat. Things looked pretty bleak in 1980, when neighboring business owner Leo LaGrotte purchased the building. Things had changed pretty dramatically in the neighborhood. Over time, the frame houses that lined College Avenue were demolished and replaced with light industry. College Avenue itself was converted to a one-way northbound street, making access to the restaurant challenging. LaGrotte envisioned knocking down the neighborhood landmark to make way for the expansion of his adjacent salvage business. Neighbors weren't too keen on this news. Through persistent badgering, they convinced Mr. LaGrotte that the restaurant could be a success with the right vision. A full-scale renovation was undertaken, adding banquet rooms to the former upstairs apartments. A new chef by the name of Vickie Dragoo came in. Under her leadership, new

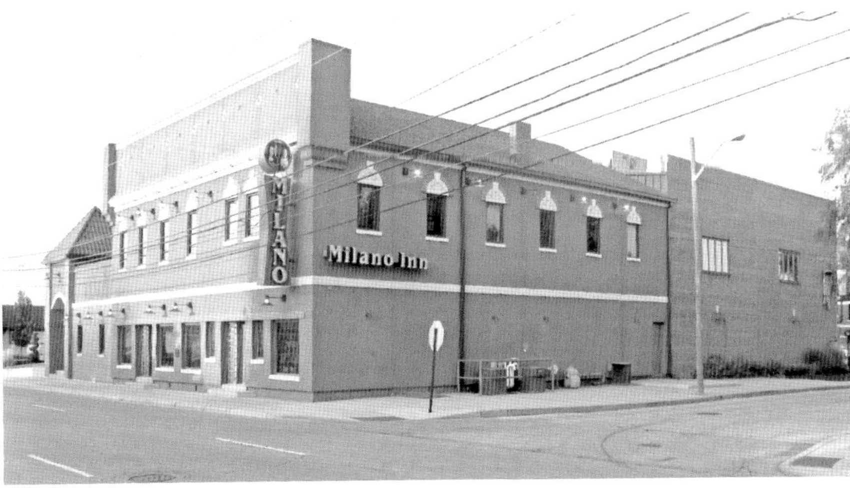

The Milano Inn has been an institution since the Great Depression. The business appeared doomed in 1980, but thankfully it was saved and expanded. *Courtesy of Jeff Kamm.*

menu items with a Northern Italian theme were added, and the restaurant became successful once again.

Today, the restaurant continues to thrive. Another major remodeling in 2010 added even more dining space, along with outdoor seating. The façade also saw some updating during construction. Under the leadership of LaGrotte's daughters, the restaurant serves as a great venue for a quiet, romantic dinner or a chilling, interactive dinner theater experience with its "Mystery Café."

Chinese

Until very recently, the Chinese population in Indianapolis had been rather sparse. The first recorded citizen hailing from the farthest of faraway lands arrived around 1880. These early Chinese served as launderers. Despite the lack of citizenry, Indianapolis served as host to a rather remarkable visitor just after the turn of the century.

In 1904, Chinese prince Pu Lun, heir to the throne, was on a tour of the United States. One of his most noted stops was his visit to the Circle City. The visit centered on a luncheon at the East Washington Street restaurant operated by Chinese immigrant Moy Kee. The establishment was closed to all regular customers that day. Great preparations were made, including Oriental rugs leading to a teakwood table along with crimson satin draperies. Oriental delicacies of every kind were served to the entourage, which included dignitaries such as Hoosier poet James Whitcomb Riley and community leader William Fortune. After the meal, the party proceeded on in what was supposed to be a caravan of automobiles from Monument Circle to Lafayette, Indiana. The start proved rather chaotic, as Fortune's car, the one the prince was supposed to embark in, caught fire. Fortunately, the drama had little effect on the visit. So impressed was Pu Lun that, upon his return, he gave restaurateur Moy Kee the "High Rank" of Chinese citizenship.

Due to wartime hostility, Indianapolis did not see a significant growth in Chinese residents until after World War II. The population was nearly all male, and little evidence of a traditional Chinese family existed. Immigration continued, and by 1990, over 1,200 Chinese lived in the city. These days, around 3,000 Chinese make their home in Indianapolis. Although early immigrants operated laundries and restaurants, today's population is almost

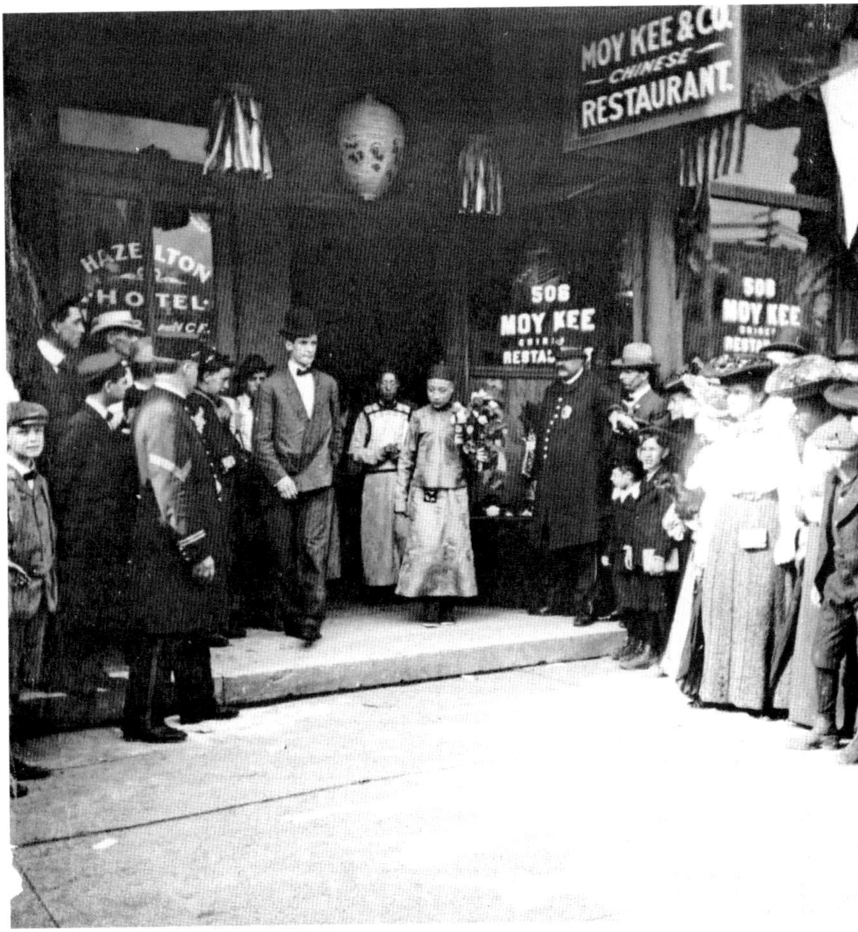

Prince Pu Lun visits the Moy Kee restaurant on East Washington Street in 1904. The building where the restaurant was located at number 508 is long gone; the site is now Harrison College. *Courtesy of the Library of Congress.*

strictly professional. Due to the sporadic nature of immigration, a true "Chinatown" has never existed in Indianapolis. That said, early Chinese restaurants tended to be clustered around the north side.

The Mandarin Inn

Despite the fact that our nation was teetering on the brink of depression in 1929, plans went forward to construct a grand building at Thirty-Eighth

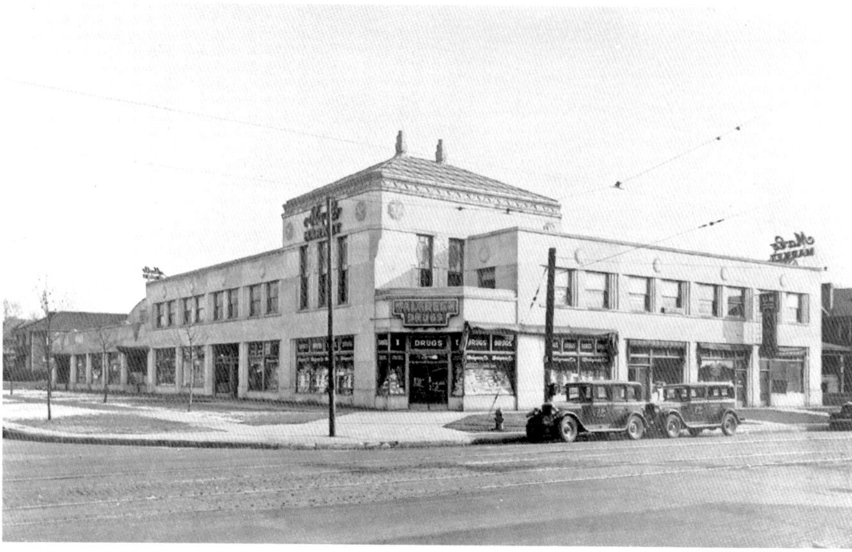

The Mandarin Inn occupied the MaCo Market Building on East Thirty-Eighth Street and was the oldest Chinese restaurant in the state until its closing in late 1980s. In a fit of irony, Walgreens, an original tenant of the MaCo Building, demolished the beautiful structure for a new suburban-style store. *Courtesy of Ball State University Library.*

Street and College Avenue. A modern design carved from Indiana limestone was promised by the Pierre and Wright architectural firm. The MaCo Marketplace, taking its name from the intersection of Maple Road (Thirty-Eighth Street) and College Avenue, would be touted as the most beautiful market building in northern Indianapolis. Ground-floor retail included the MaCo Market and Walgreens drugstore, while the above spaces included offices and studios.

During World War II, Walgreens left the Indianapolis market, creating a gaping hole in the MaCo Marketplace retail front. Chinese immigrant Danny Lee opened what would become one of the most legendary Chinese restaurants in the city in 1946. For over forty years, the Mandarin Inn served up exotic Chinese fare to hungry north-siders. After starting his restaurant, Lee would bring his family members to Indianapolis one by one, as money allowed. During this time, the restaurant gained quite a following among the Indianapolis social set. Chinese New Year celebration became an annual rite of passage.

Lee left the business in 1953, after an accounting squabble with some business partners, and started another restaurant. The Mandarin Inn was acquired by the Cheung family. Under the leadership of brothers

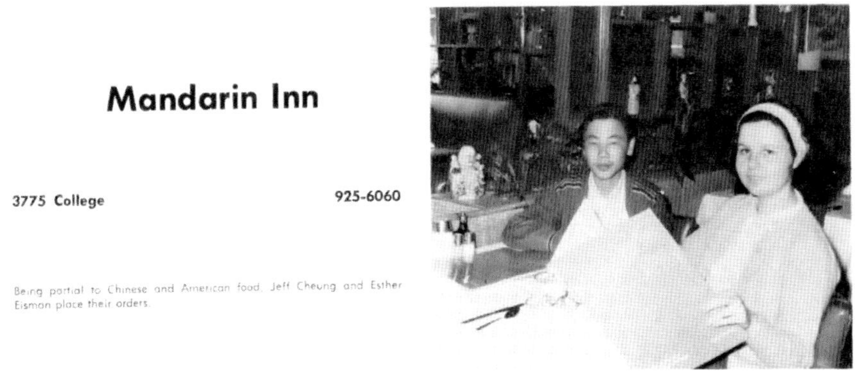

Shortridge students enjoy a meal at the Mandarin Inn. Both the restaurant and the historic building it occupied are greatly missed. *Courtesy of the Indianapolis Public Library.*

Henry and Paul, the restaurant cast a wide net to attract customers. The Cheungs brought several Cantonese dishes to the menu. Dishes like Dow Doy Yook, Charesue Fun Shee and Ming Yang Shee were available to the more adventurous Hoosiers of the time. The restaurant was also a purveyor of lobster dishes, including deviled lobster and broiled whole lobster. The Cheungs were sympathetic to the needs of the typical Indiana native, offering American fare such as a "Hong Kong steak," a broiled T-bone. The Cheung family added an all-you-can-eat buffet in the early 1980s, becoming pioneers in Chinese dining.

The Cheungs sold the business to Allen Wong in 1986; however, the good fortune and reputation of the Mandarin Inn would not continue. During this time, the MaCo building became available for sale. Developer Alan Aspinall purchased the building with the intent of remodeling the property and returning it to the intended marketplace purpose. During negotiations, a local reporter incorrectly reported that the Mandarin Inn would be closing despite the fact that Aspinall intended to honor the current lease over the next five years. Customers stopped coming, and the restaurant soon closed. Without any tenant, the building sat vacant in a state of decay. In a sick twist of fate, the property was scooped up by Walgreens, the original 1929 tenant, and demolished in 1992. Although the market portion to the east still stands, all that remains of the Mandarin portion are some salvaged limestone tiles that serve as a parking lot barrier.

Lotus Garden

After selling the popular and established Mandarin, Danny Lee didn't stay quiet for long. Along with business partner Yee Lee, he established the Lotus Garden in the newly completed Towne and Country Plaza on North Keystone Avenue. The venture opened for business on November 7, 1953. Much like the Mandarin Inn, the Lotus Garden catered to both American and Far Eastern palates. Some of the house specialties included Cantonese lobster chow mein, barbecued spare ribs, Chinese pressed duck, chicken chop suey and egg rolls. Not surprisingly for 1950s Indianapolis, the number one menu item was roast beef. In 1964, Lee introduced a new tradition to Indiana homebodies by being the first establishment to offer Chinese carryout.

Business was good on the rapidly growing north side—so good that a second outpost was deemed necessary. Lee took a gamble opening on the always underdeveloped south side. The restaurant opened in February 1965. Starting from the ground up, a truly unique dining experience was created. The local news proclaimed the restaurant to be "the most unusual of its type." To enter the dining room, one had to cross a bridge that spanned a fountain. The walls were adorned with bamboo. Aside from the main room, the "Dragon Room" was set aside for special functions. The same Chinese and American specialties that had tempted north side diners were now available to a whole new audience.

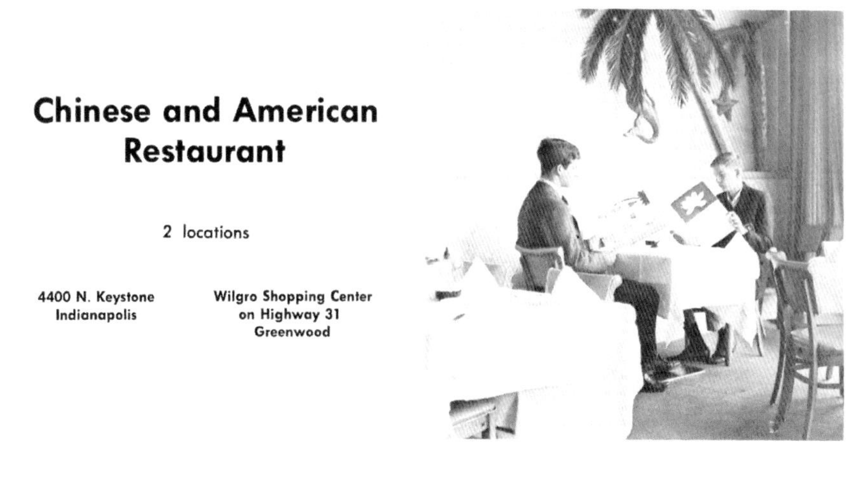

This yearbook ad shows the Indianapolis and Greenwood locations of Lotus Garden. There would also be a Carmel location that would remain open through the 1990s. *Courtesy of the Indianapolis–Marion County Library.*

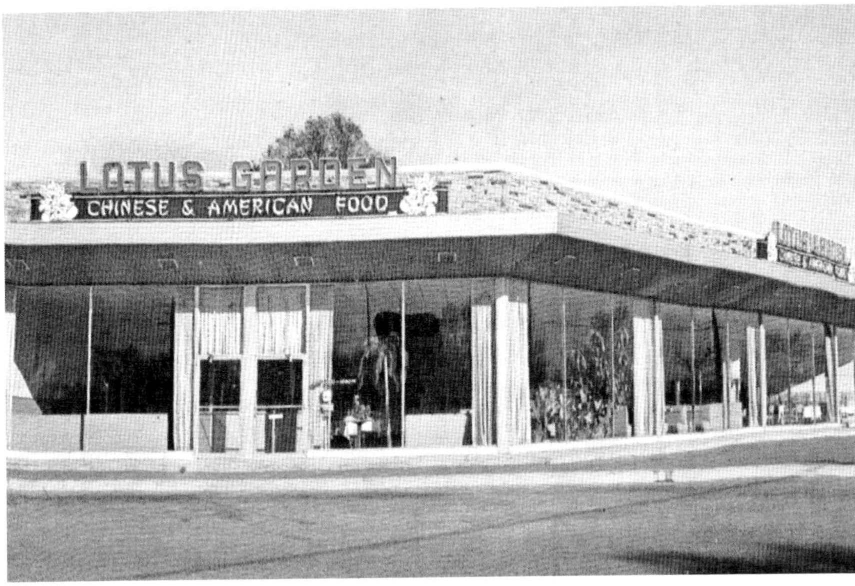

Lotus Garden had three locations at one point. This is the original, located at the Towne and Country Plaza near Forty-Sixth Street and Keystone Avenue. *Courtesy of Jeff Kamm.*

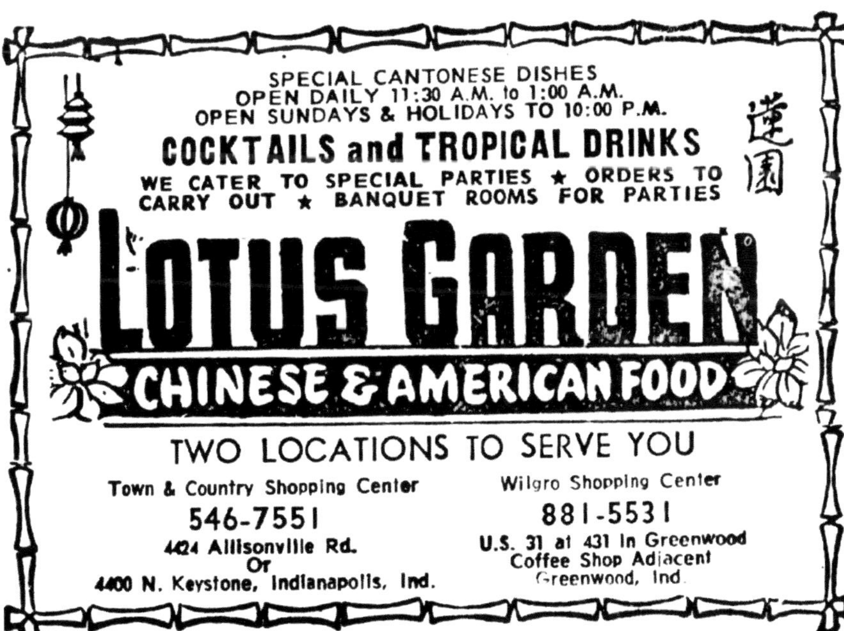

Lotus Garden proved popular and expanded to suburban Greenwood in 1965. Seven years later, a location in Carmel would also open. People can still experience this classic Chinese American restaurant in Greenwood. *Courtesy of the Indiana State Library.*

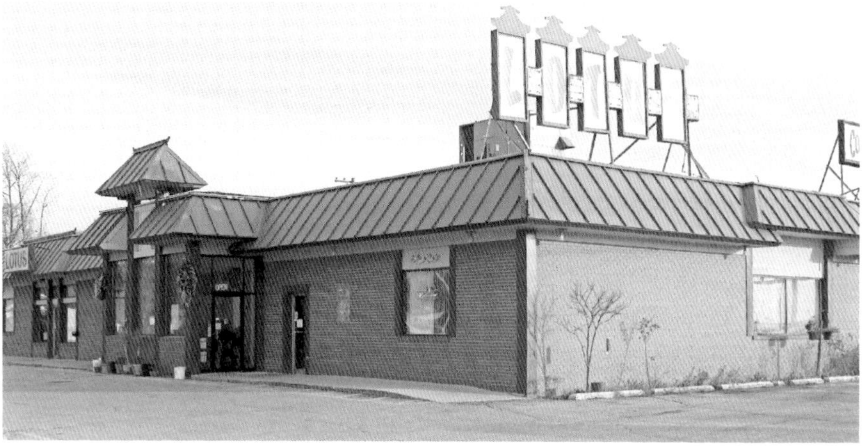

Today, the Greenwood Lotus Garden is one of the last reminders of traditional Chinese American sit-down restaurants in Greater Indianapolis. *Courtesy of Jeff Kamm.*

Several years later, a new restaurant opened on the opposite side of town. This (at the time) remote location offered a sense of mystique with its red temple gate that spanned the entrance to the parking lot. Once on the property, guests were greeted with a red pagoda trimmed in yellow and green. The grounds were lush, featuring gardens and fountains. Once inside, a red and black moon arch directed guests into the dining room. The new restaurant also featured private banquet rooms and a lounge.

With his restaurant empire spanning three sides of the city, Lee retired in 1976. The family would continue to run all three restaurants until 1999, around the time of death of the family patriarch. At this point, all three businesses were sold. The Towne and Country location closed entirely. By the 1990s, this once posh suburban shopping center had become engulfed with businesses not conducive to family dining. The Carmel location took advantage of the exotic décor and became an Asian buffet. This venture, however, was short lived. Today, the building serves as a pet boarder. One can still make out the exotic roof line, but the building is nearly inaccessible due to highway construction. Thankfully for those wanting a nostalgic sit-down Chinese experience, the Greenwood Lotus Garden soldiers on. The restaurant was purchased by the Tam family and has remained virtually unchanged. Folks on the south side swear by the food. The egg rolls are arguably the best in the city.

Jong Mea

Another long-standing Chinese restaurant landed on the near north side in February 1960 when Irving Chin opened Jong Mea. According to a blog written by a member of the Chin family, they also owned restaurants in Columbus and Mansfield, Ohio, and in Houston. The restaurant stood right on the midtown strip at 2137 North Meridian Street. The literal translation means "Chinese American," and much like the other Chinese restaurants of the time, the menu reflected that.

The restaurant liked to boast that it offered authentic Cantonese food as opposed to the heavily Americanized "Chop Suey" offered throughout the city. That said, it did cater to the non-adventurous eater by providing steaks, lamb chops, fried chicken and seafood. The signature dish, according to a 1980s advertisement, was Jong Mea Har. This combined shrimp, bacon and a sweet sauce. Most dinners were served family style, where heaping portions of entrées and sides were passed around. The restaurant was equally popular for its lunch specials. This was a quick-service options for the individual businessman looking to get in and out in a hurry.

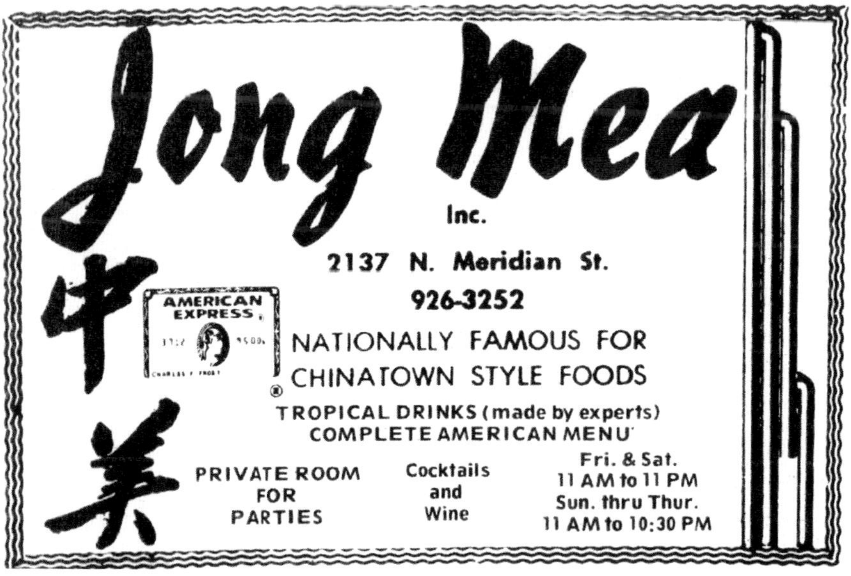

The Jong Mea on North Meridian Street was a fixture for Chinese food for forty years. The restaurant closed in 1998, and the building has since been demolished. The lot is currently vacant. *Courtesy of the Indiana State Library.*

Perhaps it was the innovations of the quick business luncheon and takeout that led to the longevity of the Jong Mea. Despite the severe decline of the neighborhood in the late 1960s, the restaurant continued to succeed. The family-owned operation finally closed in 1999, just shy of forty years. An American diner moved in briefly but did not last long. The single-story limestone building was demolished in the early 2000s; however, the vacant lot will soon be occupied by an apartment building.

Mexican

Acapulco Joe's

Directly across from one of Indianapolis's largest office towers stands a local institution. At lunchtime, officeworkers line up to savor tacos and other Mexican treats. The Hispanic population in Indianapolis has exploded over the past twenty years. As a result, many Mexican restaurants have sprung up on all sides of the city. This was not always the case. In the 1970s, a hardworking immigrant discovered a craving for fare with a South of the Border flair. This resulted in an institution that remains popular to this day. Diners still flock to the campy and comfortable Acapulco Joe's for their favorite Mexican dishes and to hear Kate Smith belt out "God Bless America" from the jukebox every day at noon.

Can you imagine risking your life and freedom so you could live out your desire for the American dream? These were stakes that a young Joe Rangel faced during the 1940s. Joe was born in San Jose, Mexico. With little opportunity in his homeland, Joe came to the United States in 1943 to work as a seasonal farmhand picking prunes in Southern California. Frustrated with the prospects of being a temporary hired hand, Joe slipped away in the middle of the night and found work washing dishes in a restaurant. Joe's liberation was short-lived, however, as he was discovered by authorities and shipped back to Mexico as an illegal alien. He would make several attempts to sneak back until 1953. This is when a federal judge became frustrated with the constant deception and sentenced Joe to six months in prison. During a bus trip, Joe was able to free himself from handcuffs and make a flying leap out of a window. He was knocked out after landing on his head and quickly recaptured. After serving his time, Joe was given seven dollars and free trip back to Mexico. Almost immediately, Joe illegally crossed the border into Texas once again, this time for good.

The language barrier resulted in Joe's arrival in the wrong "polis." On what proved to be his final trip to the United States, Joe was planning on taking a job in Minneapolis at a restaurant called Charlie's Café. Unfortunately, his English was not very good at the time. The railroad clerk sold him a ticket to Indianapolis instead. After arriving, Joe quickly discovered there was no Charlie's, and he was stranded in a strange city with no money. He reluctantly took a job at a lunch counter and began saving.

Due to Joe's hard work and charming personality, he finally had the capital to start his own restaurant. Joe's Fine Foods opened in 1961. The restaurant served a standard American menu and became successful. The year 1970 proved to be a groundbreaking one for Joe. He made a return visit to federal court, but this time it was to take his oath to become a naturalized citizen. That day, Joe posted a banner on the side of his Illinois Street eatery that proclaimed, "Now I'm a proud gringo and can raise hell about taxes like any other good citizen." As a proud new American, Joe offered free champagne to his customers. This also marked the change in his restaurant's concept. Tuesday had been a slower day, and Joe was looking for a way to attract new business. He began offering Mexican food as a weekly special. Hoosiers were quick to adapt to this strange new cuisine, and lines quickly formed down the street. The Mexican menu expanded to Wednesday, with similar results. Shortly thereafter, Joe offered a full Mexican menu every day, serving some six hundred lunch guests a day in his tiny diner.

The restaurant faced a questionable future in 1982. The American United Life Building was under construction on the other end of the block, and the company had a vision to create a sea of asphalt parking for employees in lieu of the aging, low-slung building that made up the northwest corner of downtown. Joe would fight tooth and nail to remain in the spot he had leased for twenty-one years but finally gave in. Without a clear-cut location, the future of Acapulco Joe's was very much in question. Luckily, Joe was able to settle on a location directly across the street from his now-demolished landmark. The new digs provided more seating, a bar and, for the first time, dinner hours. Although still largely successful, Joe lamented that the larger space didn't allow him to interact with the customers in the personal manner that his lunch counter had provided. The restaurant chugged along, even opening a location on the north side in 1985.

The end of an era came in 1988 when Joe Rangel passed away. The restaurant persevered under myriad subsequent owners due to the loyal

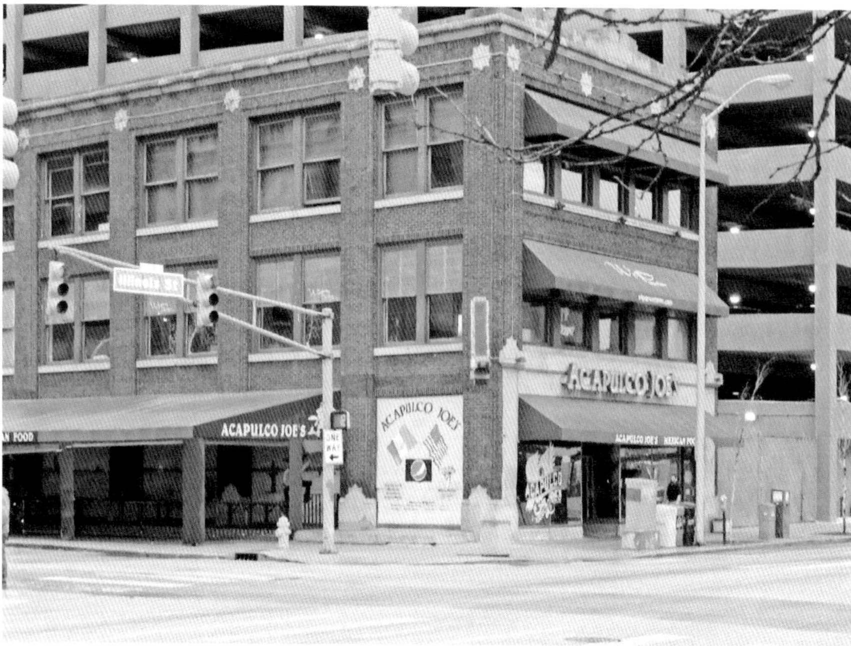

Acapulco Joe's, the venerable Mexican restaurant, still stands at the corner of Illinois and Vermont Streets. This larger version of Joe Rangel's diner opened in 1983 after the original location was purchased by American United Life Insurance. *Courtesy Jeff Kamm.*

following Joe had built throughout the 1970s and '80s. Today, the landmark is under the stewardship of Grant Redmond. Grant realized the importance of maintaining the traditions at Joe's. Over time, under different owners and with different employees, consistency lagged. Grant sought out a cook who had worked directly with Acapulco Joe himself to retrain staff on the restaurant's signature recipes. Grant has also expanded the offerings, including specials. His Baja-style fish tacos are a popular item. One complaint experienced by many first-time diners is about the salsa served with the chips. It is really more of a sweet and spicy taco sauce served from plastic bottles. The product, however, does have a strangely addictive characteristic, and changing it would seem blasphemous to longtime customers. Surprisingly enough, the most popular menu item is served up during breakfast hours. The biscuits and gravy pack heat not found anywhere else in the city. Under Grant's leadership, the restaurant is striving to reach new demographics through social media and mobile payment aps. Throughout these changing times, one can still count on a busy dining room and Kate Smith during the weekday lunch rush. Acapulco Joe's remains a true Indianapolis original.

The French Connection

When looking at the European population, it's easy to see the influence of immigrants throughout the years. The largest group, by far, were the Germans, and their influence is felt to this day. The Irish also came in large numbers beginning in the 1840s to construct our transportation infrastructure, and the Italians also maintained a noticeable presence. Surprisingly, the first settlers in the state of Indiana were the French. Primarily concerned with the fur trade, they established a series of forts along major waterways, including settlements that would become the modern cities of Vincennes and Lafayette. After the Treaty of Paris was signed in 1763, the territory came under British rule, and the French all but vanished. Although organizations such as the Alliance Française exist to promote French language and culture in Indianapolis, there are only a few modern-day businesses and festivals promoting it. This was not always the case. From the 1950s through the 1990s, a dinner in a French restaurant was seen as the ultimate experience of sophistication and romance.

Chez Jean

When heading southwest of Indianapolis toward the historic French outpost of Vincennes, travelers might notice a lonely, vacant lot strewn with gravel and fallen trees in the rapidly developing Camby area. Few would realize this was once the spot for a romantic getaway featuring the finest French cuisine in the city, served in the setting of a rustic inn. For newcomers, it seems obvious why classic French dining would not make it in this southwestern Marion County outpost. After all, the area is still somewhat rural, and folks likely feel more at ease downing comfort food at Gray Brothers Cafeteria a little farther down the road. Yet flocks of people made this trip for over fifty years to dine on escargot and other French favorites at Chez Jean Restaurant and Inn in Camby.

A twelve-room motel and restaurant serving up hamburgers and other dinner fare was commonplace along a busy highway in 1957. That changed when Jean Milesi purchased the unassuming property some twenty miles from downtown Indianapolis. Milesi, born and trained in France, had spent the previous four years working with his brother in Louisville, Kentucky, learning the ins and outs of the American restaurant business. Along with his wife, Barbara, he fashioned the motel into a destination. Patrons

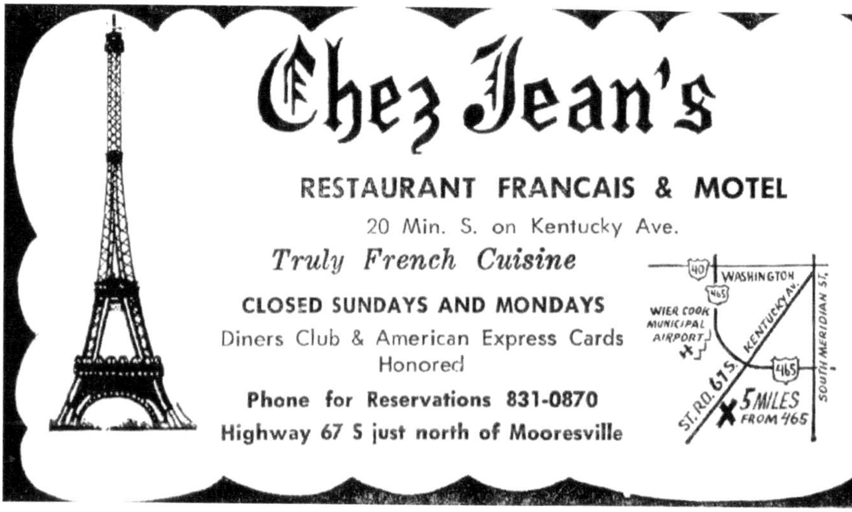

Chez Jean, located just outside the city near Mooresville, Indiana, served authentic French cuisine in a rustic, country inn setting. *Courtesy of the Indiana State Library.*

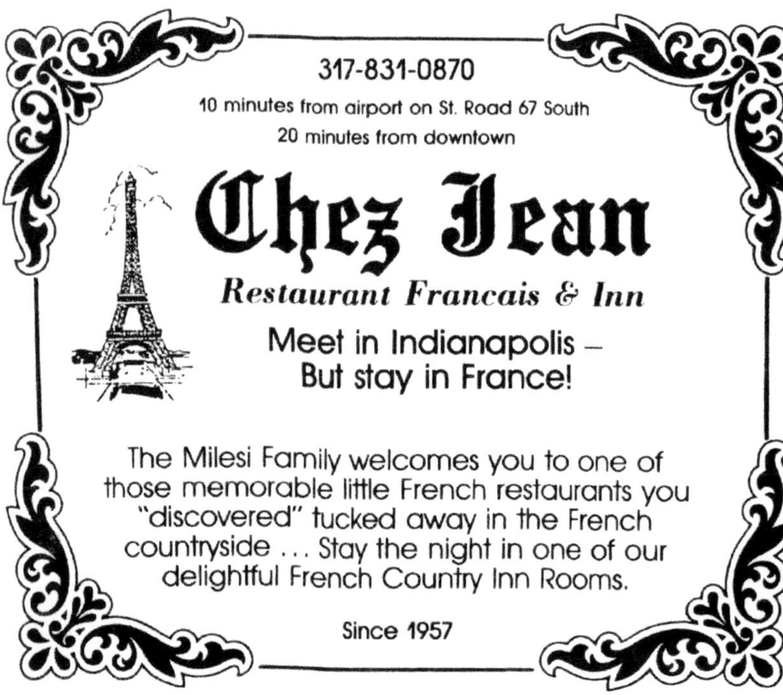

Chez Jean operated without interruption for over fifty years. Unfortunately, it couldn't survive the recession of 2008 and closed in 2009. The restaurant and inn have been demolished. *Courtesy of the Indiana State Library.*

described the experience as akin to being in the French countryside. The Milesis catered many first dates, anniversaries and high school French club outings for forty years, until they retired in 1997.

The story does not end here. Longtime family friend Chef Carl Huckaby purchased the facility from the Milesis. This brought the winner of the American Culinary Foundation's 1996 "Chef of the Year" award to the kitchen of the establishment. Huckaby was able to keep the long-standing experience that customers expected while adding to the menu. The operation expanded to include a bakery and deli on the south side of Indianapolis.

Myriad circumstances undoubtedly contributed to the demise of the venerable restaurant. The formal experience and personalized service synonymous with traditional French cuisine has become a bit passé in modern times. As higher-end restaurants with a more casual environment have sprouted up like a forest floor of mushrooms throughout recent years, the light dimmed on once sought-after destination restaurants. The collapse of the economy in 2008 was certainly no help to the profitability of the labor-intensive operation. The restaurant closed in 2009, just beating out the Chanteclair as the last traditional full-service French dining option in the area. The final guests at the property were firemen of the Plainfield Fire Department, who burned everything to the ground in a training exercise. Sadly, Chef Huckaby passed away in 2013. For a while, the sign stubbornly stood in front of the vacant lot, marking what once was, but even that has been cleared.

La Tour

While Chez Jean provided a quiet and rustic country setting, there were more sophisticated options for French dining in Indianapolis. Probably the most notable locale for budding lovers was La Tour, perched high above the Indiana National Bank Building.

The French restaurant was a go-to destination for nearly two decades. The opening of the Indiana National Bank Building in 1970 symbolized that Indianapolis was a city on the rise. The marble and glass tower rose thirty-seven stories above the street, taller than any building in the state at the time. On the thirty-fifth floor stood the flagship La Tour restaurant. Building management promised French cuisine served until 1:30 a.m. in a dining room capable of seating over 140 people, all with a spectacular view. The restaurant proved an initial hit, serving numerous gourmet luncheons and hosting many social and club events.

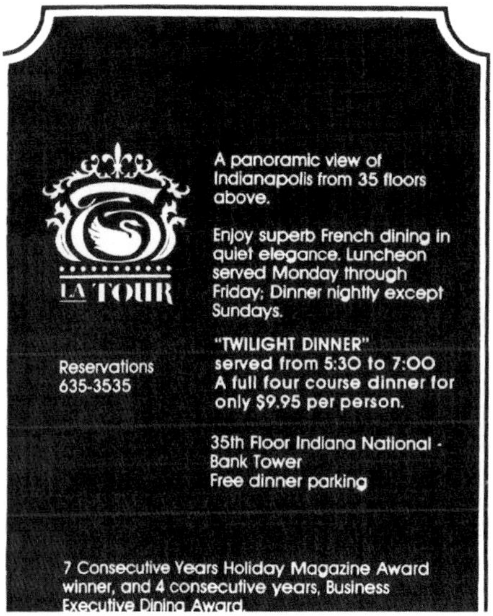

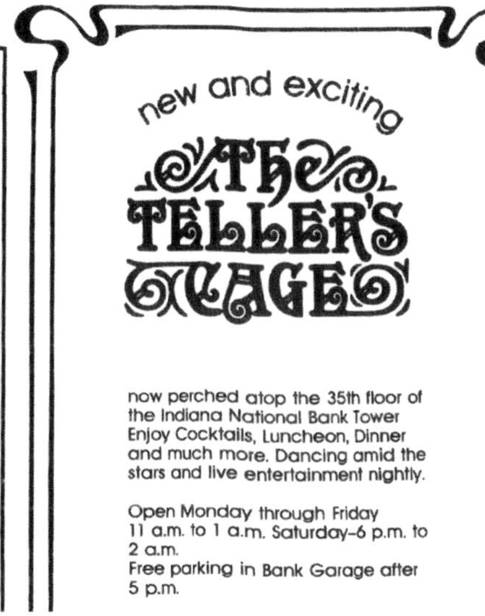

The Indiana National Bank Building featured extraordinary dining options. The La Tour restaurant was located on the thirty-fifth floor and featured the best views in the city. Originally located in the basement level, the Teller's Cage lounge eventually moved upstairs as well. *Courtesy of the Indiana State Library.*

Although unbeknownst to diners at the time, one of the first celebrity chefs took over the kitchen in 1973. Austrian Wolfgang Puck was one of three young chefs brought in from abroad. Puck elected to come to Indianapolis with the belief that it would be similar to Monaco due to the racing heritage the cities shared. Upon arrival, he was scoffed at and told people in Indiana ate only hamburgers and hotdogs. Wolfgang did tough things out for a year and established himself as the restaurant's best line cook. He was quickly off to bigger and better things, however, leaving Indianapolis for Los Angeles to create the gourmet pizza craze. By 1987, the restaurant was considered passé and in need of a change. Marriott Corporation took over the food service operations for Indiana National Bank. A full-scale renovation of the restaurant began, and French chef Allain Biller was brought in from Chicago to oversee the kitchen. This refresh ultimately proved unsuccessful. By that time, tastes were changing. Diners no longer sought out the formal atmosphere that restaurants like La Tour or the venerable King Cole offered. La Tour closed in 1989 and was replaced with the more casual Pennsylvania Street Bar and Grill. In 1992, Indiana National Bank was acquired by the National Bank of Detroit. The building suffered high vacancy rates as the local workforce dwindled. Today, Taft Law occupies the former space of La

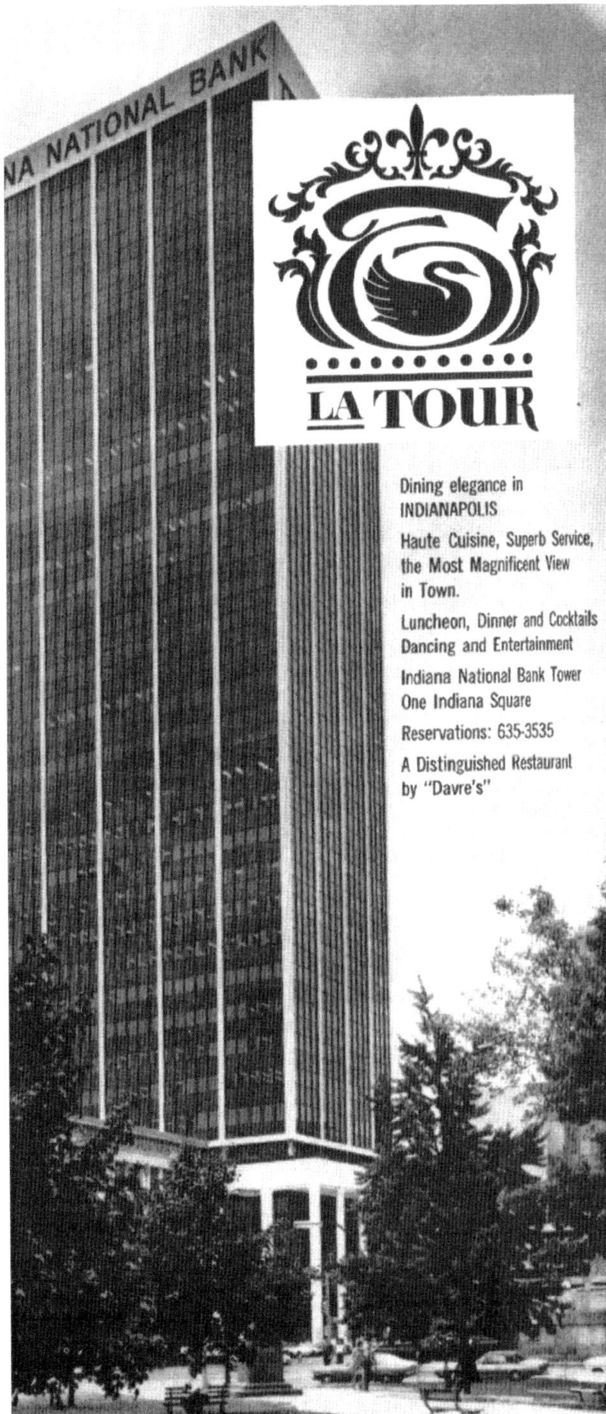

Constructed in the late 1960s and opening in 1970, the Indiana National Bank Building was the first high-rise office building in Indianapolis. *Courtesy of the Indiana State Library.*

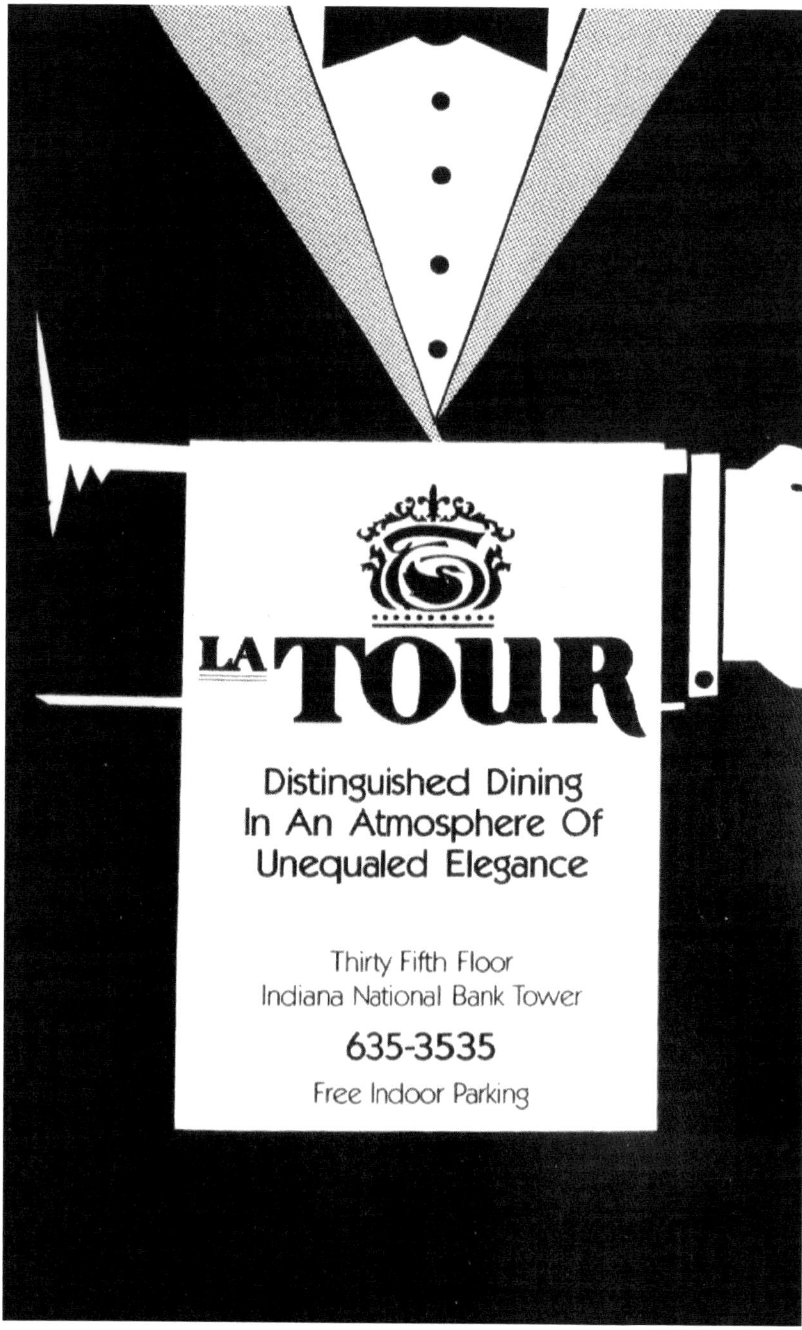

Unbeknownst to people at the time, La Tour featured a celebrity chef. Wolfgang Puck got his start in the United States manning the kitchen at this destination restaurant. *Courtesy of the Indiana State Library.*

Tour, and there is no evidence that a restaurant ever existed on the thirty-fifth floor. Wolfgang Puck would make a brief return to the city in 2004. That's when his company opened a restaurant and café at the Indianapolis Museum of Art. Due to the secluded nature of the destination, this operation was unfortunately short lived and folded in 2008.

Rene's French Restaurant

When thinking of French dining, several things come to mind. Usually, it involves an elegant dining room with tables draped in white and adorned with intricate place settings. Perhaps an image of meals served with loaves of warm, crusty bread and an endless parade of wine pairings. Offerings often include choices of exotic meat, game and fish coated in flavorful sauces whisked to perfection by chefs wearing the old uniform of all white, capped with tall white hats. Despite all of these perceived formalities, one of the first examples of French dining in Indianapolis started at a roadside motel on West Washington Street. The restaurant was known as Rene's French Restaurant.

This early Indianapolis bakery is not to be confused with Rene's French Bakery in Broad Ripple or any earlier incarnations. Rene's French Restaurant

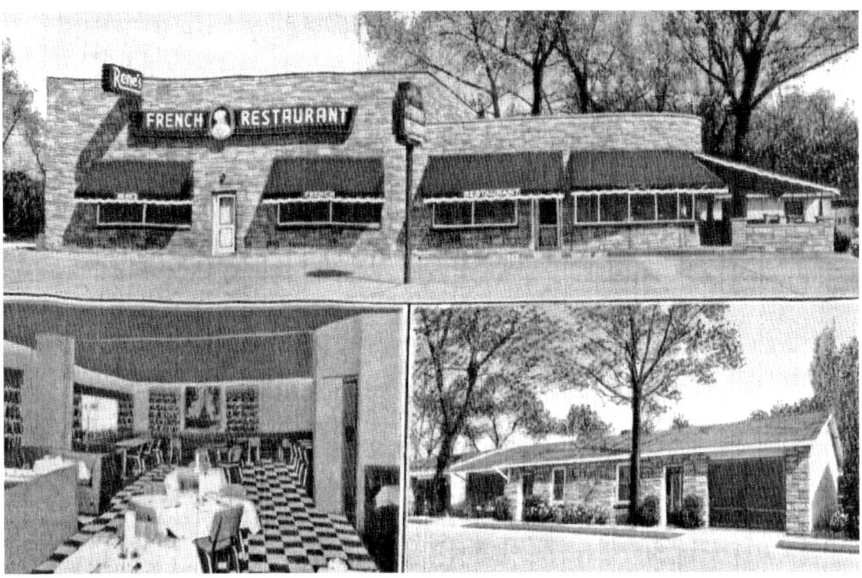

Rene's French Restaurant served up hearty meals in a nondescript building on West Washington Street. *Courtesy of Jeff Kamm.*

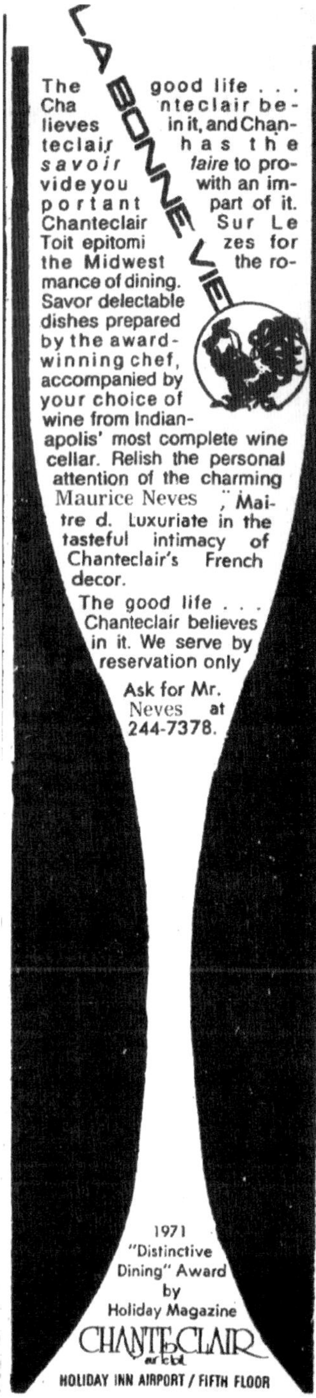

Another popular long-standing French restaurant in Indianapolis was located at the Holiday Inn at the Indianapolis International Airport. The Chanteclair closed in 2007. *Courtesy of the Indiana State Library.*

was located on a bustling U.S. 40, just east of Lynhurst Drive. The restaurant lasted approximately from the early 1950s until it ceased operations in 1963. Rene's fronted a small lodging operation known as the Eaton Motel. This would have been an excellent location for capturing transient travelers, as U.S. 40 was the bustling east–west route prior to construction of Interstate 70 in 1969.

That said, the board of fare would be a little disappointing to someone wanting a fine French meal. No traces of stereotypical dishes such as escargots and boeuf bourguignon are listed. Instead, it seems like diners were treated to cafeteria staples such as liver and onions and ham steak. It seems that even though the restaurant was founded by noted French chef Rene Milesi, tastes of Indianapolis's west side dictated what was served.

The restaurant closed in 1969, possibly not wanting to face a world without the cross-country traffic U.S. 40 once provided. All the assets were liquidated in an auction in February of that year. Today, the site of Rene's remains as only a parking lot bordered by an AT&T building and a Fazoli's location.

Chapter 5

DINERS AND DRIVE-INS

The drive-in craze in Indianapolis has faded much like the burned-out neon signs that once beckoned throngs of teenage revelers for over twenty years. Although a couple of examples can still be found, such as Mug n' Bun in Speedway and Edward's (a former Dog 'n' Suds) on the south side, they remain more as museums of nostalgia rather than as places to be seen and show off that customized hotrod.

It's hard to gauge who was the first to offer curb service in the Circle City. The concept began in 1921 in Dallas, Texas, with the opening of Kirby's Pig Stand. Numerous articles and advertisements boast that the legendary Teepee on East Thirty-Eighth Street was the first to bring one's meal to the car window; however, the Peacock, located where Massachusetts meets Thirty-Eighth, is credited as the original, according to *The Encyclopedia of Indianapolis*. The drive-in really took off after World War II as GIs returned home and mobilized to suburban areas. Soon, these establishments became a teenage rite of passage. The Indianapolis drive-in scene was territorialized based on where one went to high school. West siders attending Washington and Ben Davis would flock to the Pole on West Sixteenth Street. On the northern front, students from Short Ridge and Broad Ripple rotated around institutions such as Merrill's Hi-Decker, Borky's and, most notably, the Teepee. Those in outposts such as North Central and Carmel preferred the Northwood on U.S. 31. Tech and Howe students seemed to flock to the Steer-In, which is still serving up its classic Big Steer burger on the eastside, and the legendary Al Green's drew huge crowds from across the region with its free movies and same-day service. The south side students and Manual would not be left out, as another Teepee location opened on Madison Avenue.

Although not nearly as popular as on the East Coast, the Indianapolis area did have a couple examples of rail-car diners that surprisingly still exist today. The Oasis Diner has been lovingly restored in nearby Plainfield, thanks in part to the dedication of Indiana Historic Landmarks. The Meadowbrook, while serving as a Subway sandwich shop, still sports its shiny silver exterior on east Thirty-Seventh Street.

Drive-ins and diners in the city faced a steep decline beginning in the late 1960s. Fast-food outlets such as McDonald's and Burger Chef began to dominate the quick-serve business with their rapid-fire drive-through windows. Around this time, the original owners also retired and sold their businesses for other uses. The gas crisis in the 1970s certainly helped take the horsepower out of the teenage cruising culture, and today, all that remains of this auto-centric era is mostly memories.

The Teepee

Once the automobile age sprang up, so did campy roadside architecture. Buildings often were built in outlandish motifs to try and draw the attention of motorists whizzing by at high speeds who might be inclined to stop for a meal or a night's rest. Though some might feel these structures were garish or tacky, a growing segment of society wishes to preserve the few remaining landmarks. One of the most lamented losses in the Circle City was the famous Teepee restaurant located at the Indiana State Fairgrounds. Although the Native American theme might seem a bit offensive to today's politically correct set, the towering conical structure and hand-painted mosaics are missed by many.

The iconic Teepee restaurant opened around 1935 on the Fall Creek Parkway, on the grounds of the Indiana State Fair. The restaurant was schemed up by businessman Albert McComb and claimed to be the first drive-in in Indianapolis. The unique operation gave patrons the opportunity to dine in one of two dining rooms or in their cars or to place takeout orders. The restaurant offered over eighty items on an expansive menu that ranged from snacks to full meals. Breakfast was available at any time. Popular menu items included the Big Chief specialty hamburger and a unique salad made with a "secret" orange-colored dressing. Daily specials would

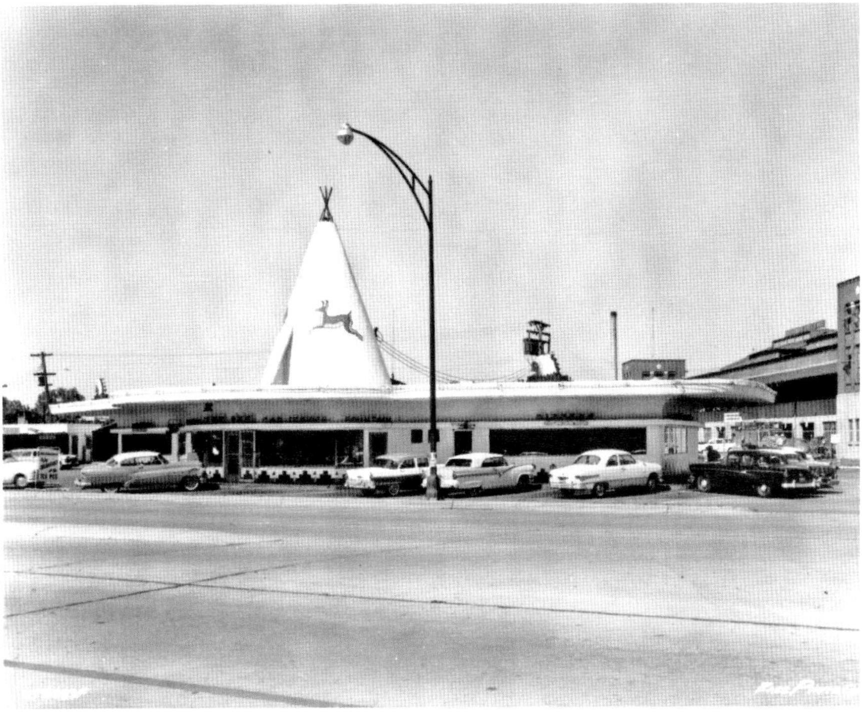

The Teepee drive-in is one of most missed restaurants in Indianapolis. After a long fight with the Indiana State Fair Board, the iconic structure was demolished in 1988. *Courtesy of the Bass Photo Company Collection, Indiana Historical Society.*

include everything from steaks to barbecue ribs and spaghetti and meatballs. Aside from all the freshly prepared entrées, the Teepee featured an in-house bakery for all breads and pastries served, including its trademark strawberry pie. McComb must have been doing something right, as the restaurant flourished despite the Depression and World War II.

After the war years, the restaurant really took off. Returning GIs appreciated the quick and casual curb service. Before long, area teenagers and Butler University students discovered the pointed landmark, and the Teepee became the place to be seen on weekend nights. Due to the popularity of the north side location, the tribe set up shop on South Madison Avenue in 1955. The sister restaurant offered an updated Native American motif and the same great menu. As crowds surged, yet another location in Nora opened up. However, change was brewing.

Albert McComb passed away in 1964, shortly after the opening of the Nora store. As the 1960s wore on, the once popular drive-in culture was

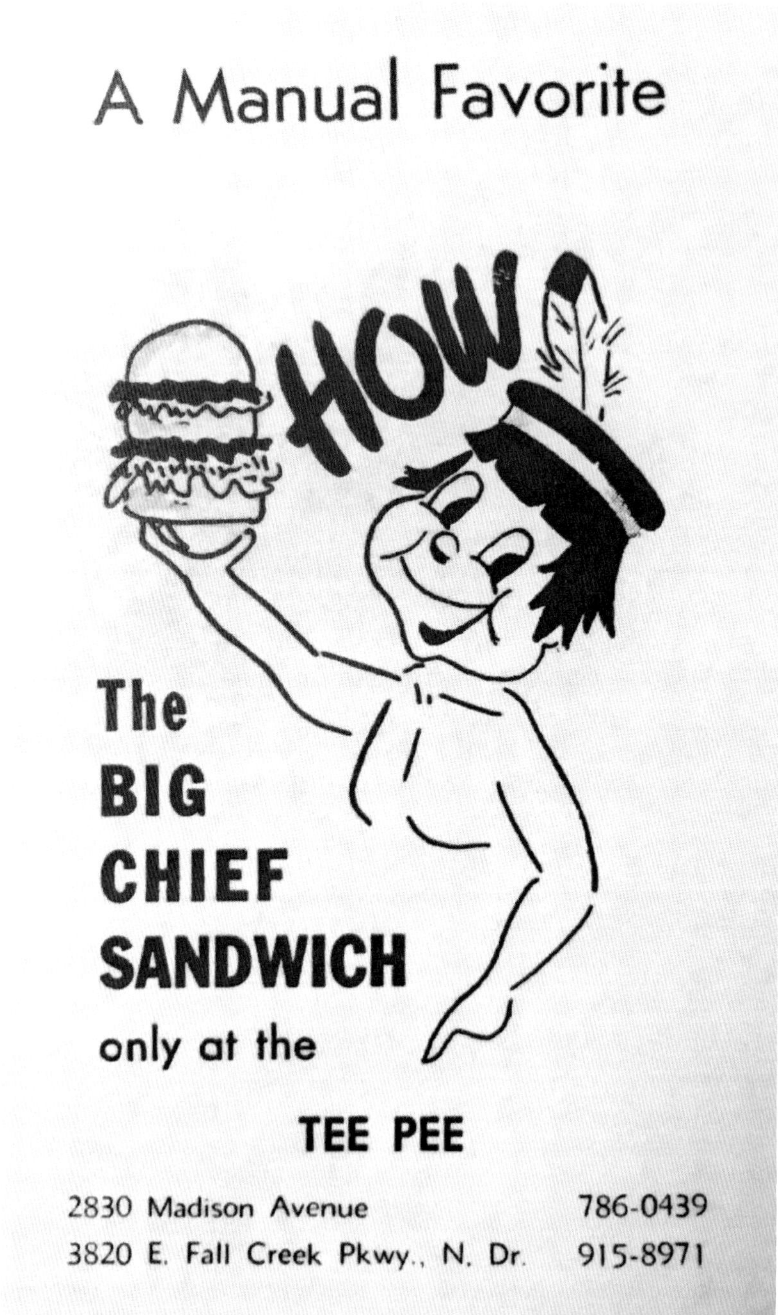

This cartoon Indian advertised the Big Chief double-decker sandwich. The Teepee was also famous for its strawberry pie. *Courtesy of the Indiana State Library.*

fading. Fast-food outlets such as McDonald's and Burger Chef were taking over the quick-serve landscape. The Nora Teepee was the first to succumb to changing trends. McComb's widow continued to operate the remaining two locations through the 1970s; however, the once trademark curb service ceased. The south side location succumbed to changing tastes in 1979 to become the site of a McDonald's, and the McComb family closed the fairgrounds location shortly thereafter.

The restaurant was given a second chance at life after shuttering. In 1981, new owner Dick Turner attempted a revival. He maintained the original Teepee menu, offering freshly made foods and the "best steaks in the city at the best prices." Unfortunately, this new venture proved to be in vain. By 1982, the State Fair Board of Directors, which owned the whole reservation, elected to demolish the historic structure to create more parking spaces. This forced Turner into bankruptcy and awoke a tribe of historical preservationists wishing to save the roadside landmark. The fight ensued for nearly seven years, and many held out hope that the decaying edifice would survive and perhaps serve to function as an information center for the Indiana State Fair. The restaurant became a memory as crews demolished the Teepee in June 1988. For a while, Turner gave hints of a rebirth on the south side, as he had acquired the rights and recipes of the original restaurant, but those smoke signals have all but dissipated. The only trace of the Teepee today is in the memories of the generations who enjoyed the food and fellowship of an Indianapolis icon.

The Pole

Another landmark drive-in still stands on the near west side, even if its days serving up snacks and confectionaries have long since passed. One might think that an establishment just a couple miles east of the Indianapolis Motor Speedway would take on the name "the Pole" in tribute to that coveted starting position for the annual Indianapolis five-hundred-mile race, but that would be a bit presumptuous.

What would become the Pole featured a familiar cast of characters in Indianapolis drive-in lore. The restaurant began in 1930 at a completely different location. The North Pole opened in the picturesque Butler Tarkington neighborhood near the intersection of Illinois and Fifty-Sixth Streets, taking a frigid name to promote the frozen custard that would become the soda fountain's trademark. The restaurant was started by Pop Spencer, who was an Indianapolis drive-in pioneer. Spencer also operated the Northwood Drive-In, along with a sit-down restaurant on Allisonville Road. The location was a popular spot for Shortridge students to cool off on hot summer days.

By 1952, Spencer had handed all day-to-day business operations to his protégé, William "Merle" Agner. Perhaps Agner was displeased with his ability to expand in the quiet north side neighborhood, or maybe he saw the tremendous opportunity of having a restaurant located between Victory Field and the Indianapolis Motor Speedway. Whatever the motivation, Merle decided to close the long-term landmark and move to a completely different side of town. He purchased the parcel where Lafayette Road spilled all the traffic coming from Chicago onto West Sixteenth Street with the intention of opening a massive drive-in with parking for some four hundred cars. Originally, he wanted to call the new digs Merle's but opted to maintain ties to the former location, settling on the Pole. The new location soon became the epicenter for west side social life and served as a gathering spot to celebrate victories during the state basketball tournament.

The Pole remained a popular spot through the 1960s, but as the decade ended, Agner was ready to relax. Having sold his Northwood operation to Frisch's a few years earlier, Agner put the Pole up for sale at the end of the 1969 season. Unable to attract a restaurant tenant, the location has served as a used vehicle dealer ever since that time. Today, an operation specializing in work trucks and vans is taking advantage of the massive parking lot to showcase its products.

Merrill's Hi-Decker

During the age of flattops and dungarees, catching the fickle fancy of area teenagers was the crux of local drive-in operators. Many outlandish gimmicks were hashed out to keep the parking lots packed full. One of Indianapolis's legendary drive-ins was a rather short-lived venture. However, due to a New York import, it proved to be one of the spots to be seen in the late 1950s. The venture came about as a tale of two restaurants.

The main drag on the north side of the city has historically been Thirty-Eighth Street—or Maple Road, as it was known in early times. The wide boulevard originally started at Michigan Road, guiding motorists past the

Indiana State Fairgrounds to the Fall Creek Parkway and points east. This proved to be an excellent location for a restaurant, and W.L. McGinley took advantage. He constructed one of the finest restaurant buildings of the time directly across from the main entrance to the fairgrounds. The building was unique, featuring a circular, multi-level dining room that was an honorable mention for the Indiana Architectural Records' "Most Outstanding Recent Building" Award in 1940. McGinley also operated several other Parkmoor restaurants in Greater St. Louis. The locations featured curb service, which was coming into vogue at the time, along with takeout meals of its famous Dixie Chicken. Business must not have been too brisk, as the restaurant closed quietly in 1954.

Meanwhile, downtown, another restaurateur was busy carving out his niche. Merrill Cohen was riding high, operating two restaurants in the largest office buildings of the time. Cohen operated cafeterias in the Chamber of Commerce Building and the Hume Manser Building, along with a catering business. Known for being an innovator in the restaurant business, Cohen saw opportunity when it was announced that Purdue University would be opening an extension next to the shuttered Parkmoor. Cohen quickly scooped up the hot property and reopened the drive-in as Merrill's Hi-Decker. The restaurant had a rather quiet existence, serving as a hangout for Shortridge and Broad Ripple students. This all changed in 1958.

A new face for the Hi-Decker arrived in 1958; however, this wasn't a pretty carhop or a salty old line cook. Dick Summer came to local radio heavyweight WIBC from Brooklyn, New York. The dynamic young disc jockey soon struck a deal with Cohen to broadcast live from the drive-in on a nightly basis. The "Skyline Studio" was constructed atop the unique round building, giving Summer a perch from which to conduct his symphony of 1950s teenage antics. The program, dubbed *Summer Time*, was broadcast nightly from 9:15 p.m. until 1:00 a.m. The program featured personal interviews with members of the "Skyline Club," along with contests and scavenger hunts. One of the most memorable stunts came just after the ten o'clock news break. That's when Summer held his "Make It or Break It" contest. A record from an emerging artist, often local, was played to the jury of parked cars for approval. One could voice his or her opinion by honking the car horn. If the record was a "make," the tune would be played once an hour for an entire week. More often, the result was not so positive. If panned by the parking lot critics, Summer would promptly smash the record over his microphone—to the delight of the crowd. In a recent blog entry, Summer reminisced about a manager who hated one tune with such fervor that he fired a handgun toward the Skyline Studio. It was merely a blank round, but Summer would get the last laugh. The next evening, he wedged a block of Limburger cheese into the engine block of the would-be marksman's car, creating a rather unpleasant olfactory experience for the driver and occupants.

Riding high off the success of *Summer Time*, Dick would move on to a larger radio station in St. Louis, leaving the Hi-Decker without a gimmick. The crowds dwindled at the restaurant, causing Cohen to utilize cars from a nearby dealer to give the appearance of a happening joint. The high-traffic site was eventually sold to the Burger Chef chain, which demolished the drive-in in favor of one of its boilerplate fast-food restaurants. This location survived the Hardee's takeover; however, by the late '80s, concerns of crime in the area had scared away most customers. The fairgrounds eventually bought up all the land south of Thirty-Eighth Street and cleared away everything for parking.

This would not be the end of Merrill Cohen. After the Hi-Decker fell from grace, he invested heavily in the then thriving Meadows area of Indianapolis, opening a cafeteria in the expansive shopping center and providing food service for the brand-new Avondale Dinner Theater. Cohen would go into the theme restaurant business, opening two Stockholm House Scandinavian-themed restaurants in the Meadows and at Eastgate that remained successful throughout the 1970s, and he maintained his catering business through the 1980s.

Al Green's Famous Food

"A one-stop shop for everything 1950s culture" best describes Al Green's Famous Food, an eastside landmark for forty years. Teens would flock to the bright-pink building fronted by a huge neon sign. This was a true hangout. Embracing the leisurely nature of the operation, the restaurant's slogan boasted "same-day service." Customers could snack on huge portions of fried fare, all while taking in a movie or live music. Although our fast-paced world has made joints like this completely obsolete, folks from the era still speak about cruising Al's with a glimmer in their eyes, recalling the food, fun and caring owners who would let them hang out even if they didn't have a dime to spend.

Al opened his drive-in shortly after returning home from World War II in 1947. Originally, he scouted for land close to downtown but grew tired of not being able to find enough acreage. Eventually, he settled on "the center of nowhere," along U.S. 40 on the far east side of Indianapolis. Al, his brother Nathan and their sister Belle took advantage of the location, hosting hungry cross-country travelers. The focus was on "jumbo" items. A simple order of French fries would be four times the size of a competitor's. The mammoth breaded tenderloin was referred to as "the half hog." When you ordered the chicken, you received precisely that: an entire chicken. As the auto age expanded, Al found his business cut off by the newly constructed Shadeland Freeway. Thumbing his nose at the new obstacle, Al constructed what was rumored to be the largest illuminated sign in the country to beckon to customers. The green and yellow behemoth would be a landmark for over forty years. Al was also a pioneer in technology. During the drive-in's heyday, he installed the world's first two-way telephone-ordering system. Consisting of some 160 phone lines and a switchboard complete with operator, the system helped the carhops manage the more than four hundred cars of hungry students from schools such as Warren Central, Howe, Arsenal Tech and Shortridge. Al took the drive-in to the next level by installing a movie screen and speakers. Al's brother Nate would man the projection booth, showing hours of cartoons followed by second-run movies. Bands would play often, and radio stations such as WIBC would broadcast on-site. If ever there was a capital for cruising culture, Al Green's surely had to be it.

Unfortunately, by the late 1960s, the world was no longer accepting the "who cares," leisurely attitude embraced by the Greens. Fast-food franchises became the norm on the growing east side, and business slowed. The movie projector went silent in 1974. By 1976, the restaurant had taken another hit when Al's brother Nathan passed away. Lunch hours were scrapped, and the drive-in opened only twice a week—although later it would expand back to seven. By this time, the giant sign was no longer lit up at night, and many assumed the restaurant had closed.

By the time the mid-1980s rolled around, Al Green's stood more as a monument to nostalgia than an actual working restaurant, becoming a gathering spot for local car clubs, whose members were allowed to hang out on the grounds. The throngs of teenagers were long gone, with the newer generation moving on to other diversions. The outdoor movie screen was silenced, and most of the lights were burned out. Still, this did not deter Al and his sister Belle from greeting and serving old friends who stopped by to reminisce. Couples, now married for over thirty years, would come by to celebrate their first dates. By now, the "same-day service" motto held true. Diners often waited patiently, often for over two hours, to receive their orders; the experience was more about the memories and conversations.

For a time, it seemed that Al Green's would go on forever, but it just wasn't meant to be. Al and Belle would retire and close up shop in 1985, ending an era of Indianapolis history. For the next decade, the dilapidated restaurant stood just west of Shadeland Avenue as a reminder of a bygone era that will never be relived. Al passed away in April 1996. Perhaps it's fitting that he never had to endure the pain of seeing his teenage empire crumble; however, time marches on. The little pink octagon was finally cleared away in 1997. Today, the site is home to a Hyundai dealership.

Northwood Drive-In

In mid-century Indianapolis, nobody thought much about what lay north of the White River. This barrier served as a boundary for the city, and nothing but fields and forests lay beyond. That began to change in the early 1950s as Washington Township began to develop as an exclusive address. The area of Nora saw tremendous growth, and by 1956, a new high school was deemed necessary to house all of the poodle skirts and saddle shoes of the day. The go-to hangout for these North Central Panthers was a little drive-in located near the county line on U.S. 31 known as the Northwood.

The little stucco building was not only the social epicenter for North Central students but also served as a cruising spot for kids from the farming communities of Carmel and Zionsville. The restaurant was operated by Indianapolis drive-in pioneer Samuel Spencer, who also operated another hotspot called the North Pole on Illinois Street. By 1948, the operation had been taken over by William Agner, who saw the boom of cruising culture. Business was so good that an expansion was in order. Agner demolished the early 1940s structure and constructed a modern drive-in, complete with covered car stalls, in 1962. Shortly thereafter, Agner was able to relax a little as Frisch's Big Boy, out of Cincinnati, eyed the spot for one of its area outlets. The operation was leased, and the iconic Big Boy statue stood guard over North Meridian.

The Frisch's restaurant group has had a love-hate relationship with the Circle City over the years, starting with carnivorous expansion only to be followed by a sudden and complete retreat from the market. Such was the case the first time the chain left in 1969. For the next two decades, the

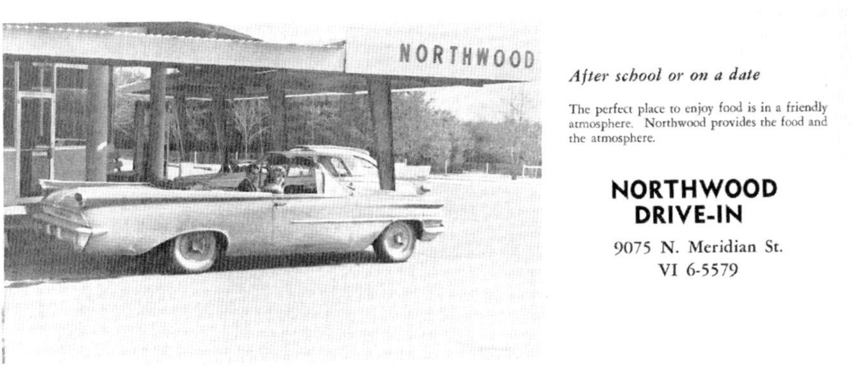

The Northwood Drive-In was another popular cruising spot for many years. The location would serve as a Frisch's Big Boy in the 1960s and would be known by several other names until around 1988. A Tucker real estate office now sits on the former site on the far north side. *Courtesy of the Indianapolis–Marion County Library.*

Northwood location would feature an ever-changing lineup of restaurants; however, by the late 1980s, the area had evolved into sleek office buildings and upscale housing. The humble drive-in met its fate with the wrecking ball around 1990 to make way for a real estate office. William "Merle" Agner passed away in February 1996.

The Huddle

A twenty-four-hour restaurant tends to bring out some of the more interesting examples of mankind—especially in the wee hours of the morning. A mix of shift workers, college procrastinators and weekend revelers trying to sober up on coffee and greasy fare can be found in the vinyl-clad booths in area restaurants such as Steak 'n' Shake, Denny's and IHOP. While today's examples tend to be corporate giants, Indianapolis once had a local destination where locals satisfied those 3:00 a.m. omelet cravings.

The Huddle Restaurants (not to be confused with the Georgia-based Huddle House) proudly boasted breakfast all day at locations on every side of the city. Founded in the 1950s by Orville Stonebreaker, these family-style restaurants were often paired with Haag Drugstores, much like the Knife & Fork relationship with Hook's Drugs. Featuring a long stool-lined counter, hot coffee and a menu full of greasy delights, a Huddle would be the perfect oasis for the night owl. This local chain had restaurants at Fifty-Sixth and

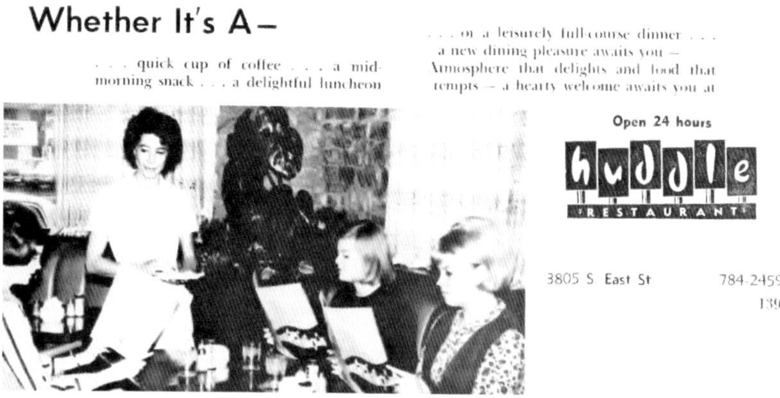

Huddle restaurants were located all around Indianapolis, often alongside Haag Drugstores. They served as popular twenty-four-hour spots to grab a bite. *Courtesy of the Indianapolis–Marion County Public Library.*

Illinois Streets, Devington Plaza, Twin Aire Plaza, Sixty-Second Street and Keystone Avenue and in Nora. The midtown location at 2034 North Meridian had to be hopping when the adjacent Ember's Nightclub let out during the early 1960s.

The restaurants were popular throughout the '60s and are still fondly remembered by residents of that era, despite their fade into obscurity. By 1975, city directories listed the Twin Aire as the sole remaining location, and by 1976, even that was gone. In 1979, the Illinois Street Food Emporium opened in the former Huddle at Fifty-Sixth and Illinois Streets, where it continues to thrive today. Most of the shopping centers are still around in some form, though the Meridian Street location consists of only cars for workers at Citizens Energy. Haag's Drugs had been purchased by People's Drugs by 1980 and was later consumed by CVS. The Stonebreaker family is still active in the restaurant business as owners of the longtime favorite Murphy's Steakhouse at Fifty-Second Street and Allisonville Road.

The Oasis Diner

Sometimes you just can't stop progress. As the sprawl of Indianapolis spreads farther past the boundaries of Marion County, small, independent communities are constantly gobbled up, along with their identities. Recently,

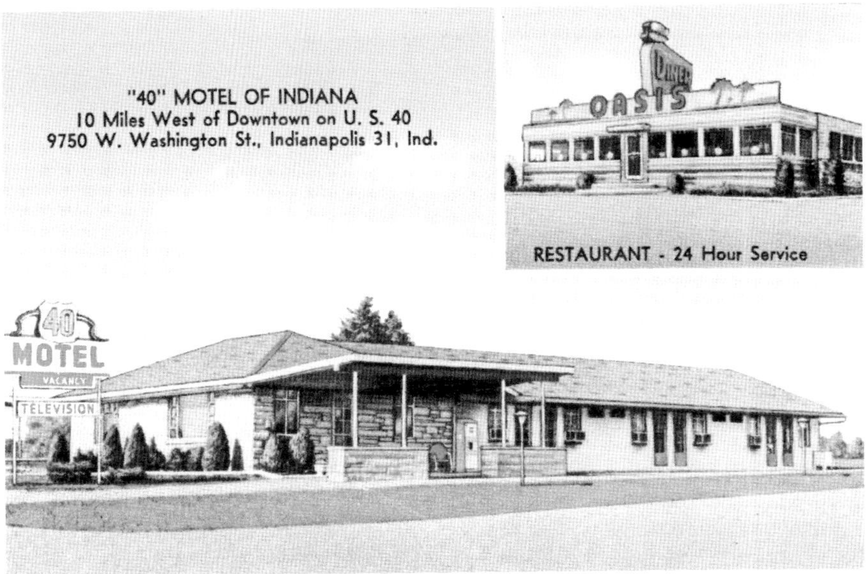

This postcard shows the Oasis Diner and adjacent 40 Motel. Both were located on the far west side of Indianapolis in a tiny community known as Six Points. *Courtesy of Jeff Kamm.*

this has happened to a west side crossroads known as Six Points. The area known as Six Points can trace its history back to 1851, during the construction of the Terre Haute and Indianapolis Railroad. The railroad crossed the old National Road near the Marion and Hendricks County lines, at the intersection of another north and south road, creating a six-pointed intersection. This setup had the potential to create havoc with horses of both the natural and the iron variety. By 1925, the automobile had become commonplace, and the once nearly deserted National Road became part of the new United States Highway System. As traffic increased, the six-pointed intersection proved to be a treacherous liability.

To handle all of the new traffic, the State of Indiana began widening U.S. 40 between 1936 and 1943. The Six Points area was completely bypassed by a new four-lane highway that included an overpass across the railroad. Businesses took advantage of the advantageous location between Indianapolis and Plainfield. Several motels popped up, complete with flickering neon signs. In 1954, the iconic Oasis Diner was shipped in from New Jersey by rail. The prefabricated unit was known as a Mountain View–style diner. The location proved successful as an oasis for weary travelers. Despite being completely bypassed once again in 1969 by Interstate 70, the diner remained intact thanks to a steady stream of regular customers.

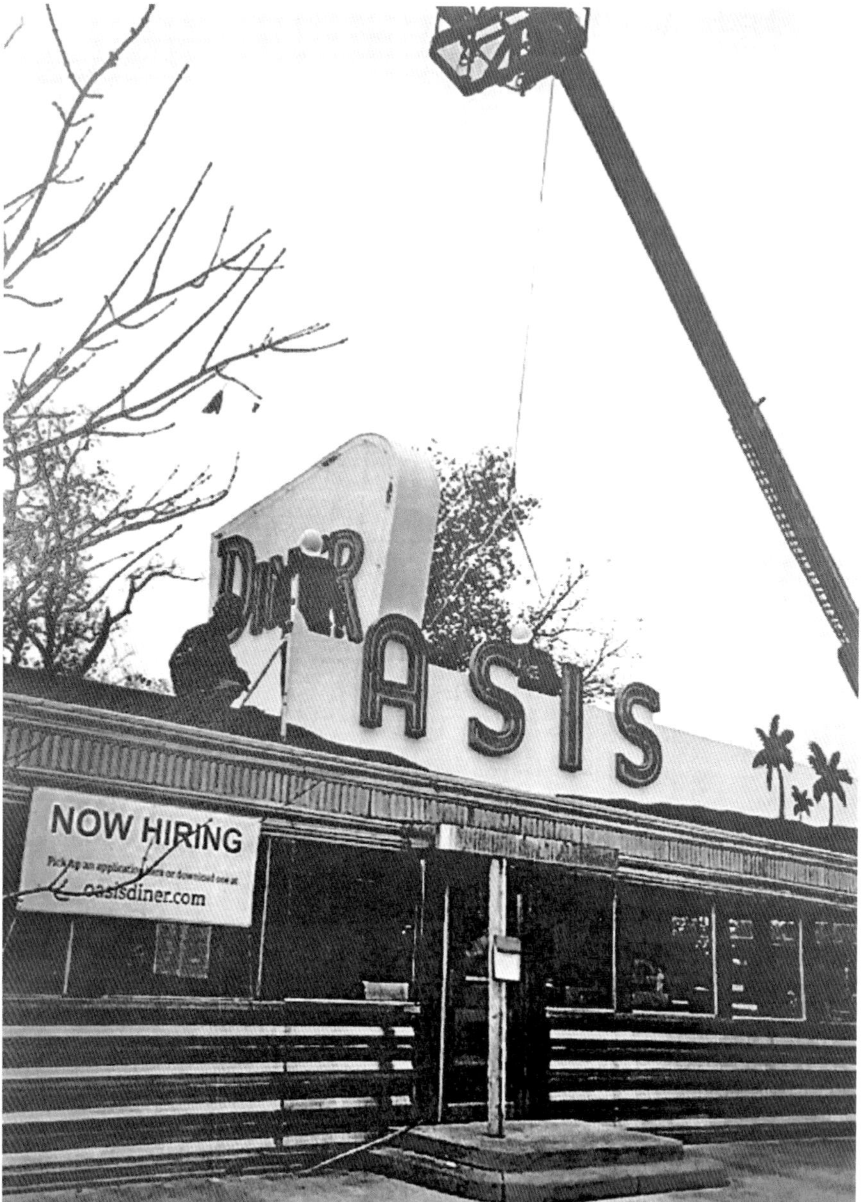

The finishing touches are placed atop the relocated diner. The diner was relocated to nearby Plainfield after several years on the "Ten Most Endangered Structures" list distributed by Indiana Historic Landmarks. *Courtesy of Doug Huff.*

The business, known for its breaded pork tenderloins, survived three owners relatively intact through the 1990s.

Things would begin to change for the silver roadside landmark. Throughout the 1990s, the Indianapolis International Airport expanded, buying up nearly all of the property between the Marion County line and the eastern Hendricks County community of Plainfield. In the place of farms, homes and small businesses, giant warehouses and industrial complexes sprang up like dandelions in the spring. The area was ripe for development due to its location near the airport and access to major highways. Things looked pretty bleak for the diner in 2009. That's when the county condemned the structure, citing concern over a leaky foundation in the rear limestone. The iconic building that had served generations of travelers had been placed on the Indiana Historic Landmarks' "Ten Most Endangered Structures" list by 2010.

Luckily, things worked out for all involved. Due to the publicity the endangered building received, the Town of Plainfield began to look for a

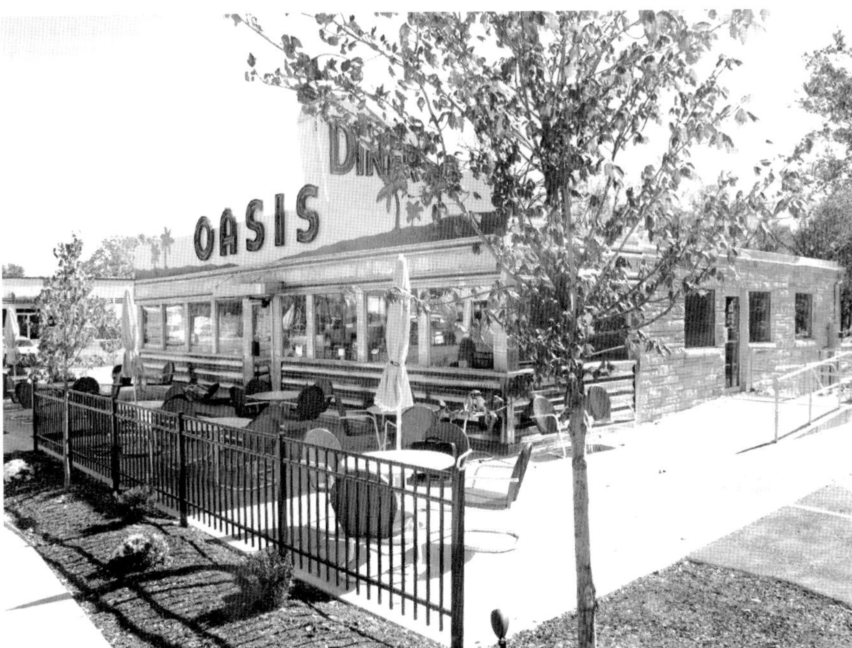

The fully restored Oasis Diner features many of the classic menu items for which it was known, along with unique daily specials. *Courtesy of Jeff Kamm.*

solution. It began to study grant possibilities to keep the building on U.S. 40. Local contractor Doug Huff became involved in moving the entire location a few miles down the road to the heart of Plainfield's historic district. This proved to be a three-and-a-half-year process. The rear portion of the building was a permanent structure made of Indiana limestone. Unfortunately, this had already been sold for reuse, and a replica had to be created. In August 2014, amid much local interest, the rail car portion or the diner crawled slowly down U.S. 40 to its new home to the west. By November, everything had been put back together, and Mr. Huff was ready to usher in the next era of the diner.

These days, the only difference between the building and the original photos is the location. All of the neon signage and bright-yellow trim has been restored to the original condition. Doug has kept many of the original menu items; however, he has enhanced the offerings. These days, the operation bakes all of its own breads and desserts. Favorite items include the Oasis Burger, featuring a half pound of beef along with pulled pork and bacon. The diner also offers weekly specials, oftentimes featuring items not typically associated with a roadside outpost, such as shrimp and grits. Like at any good diner, twenty-four-hour breakfast is a mainstay. People flock for the Kansas City loaded biscuits and gravy. This all-in-one dish is topped with two eggs, home fries, crumbled bacon and cheddar cheese.

Customers tell Mr. Huff that their favorite aspect of the Oasis Diner is the memories it brings back of the original location and how happy they are that a tradition has been preserved for the next century. With its great location next to a youth sports park and motivated staff, the Oasis Diner looks poised to continue the tradition of serving up comfort food along one of America's iconic highways.

Knobby's Drive-In

One of the longest-standing restaurants in Indianapolis stood on Keystone Avenue for nearly half a century. What was for many years a legendary, local diner that served up breakfast, lunch and dinner started out as a teenage hotspot in a completely different location.

Knobby's Drive-In was the dream of World War II veteran William A. Knoll. The Connersville native was stationed mostly in the South Pacific during the conflict, serving in the U.S. Navy. After spending a couple of years working at Naval Avionics, Knoll decided to become his own boss. He opened Knobby's

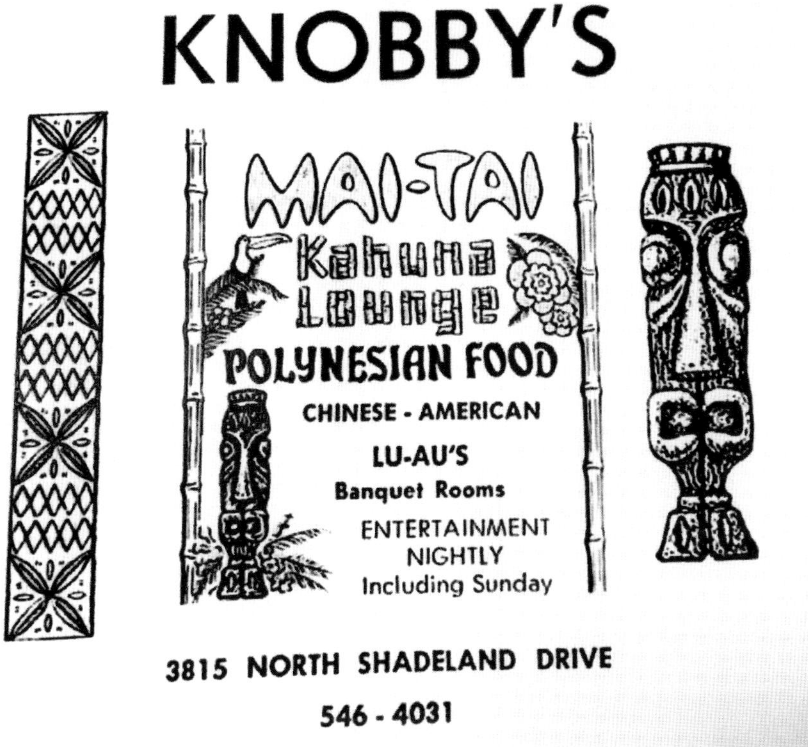

Knobby's at one time featured three locations. A change in the business model spelled an end to curb service and a shift to more traditional dining. The original on Keystone Avenue lasted until 2001. Today, a BP gas station stands on the site. The Shadeland Avenue location later housed a karate school but now stands abandoned. *Courtesy of the Indiana State Library.*

in 1951, right across from the fairgrounds. East Thirty-Eighth Street must have been quite the scene in the 1950s, with Knobby's, the Parkmoor and the Teepee all within a stone's throw. Business must have been good. Knoll opened a second location farther down Thirty-Eighth Street in 1954, and the following year he opened what would become his flagship store at Keystone and Fifty-Second.

Perhaps it was memories of the South Seas that caused Knoll to drastically change his business model in the mid-1960s. The restaurateur kicked the carhops to the curb and gained liquor licenses for his establishments. The greatest change was at the Shadeland Avenue location. Sporting a Polynesian theme, the restaurant was renamed the Mai-Tai. The adjacent Kahuna Lounge specialized in large, fruit-filled, Tiki-style drinks.

By 1978, Knoll had all but retired, leaving the restaurants to his sons, Tom and Andrew. Shortly thereafter, Andrew moved to Mississippi, spelling the end of

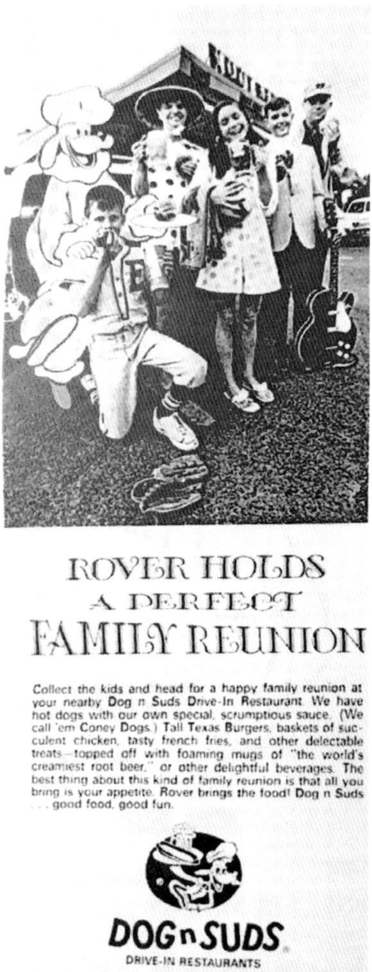

I would be remiss if I didn't mention the Dog 'n' Suds chain of restaurants. Started by two Illinois teachers, the restaurant chain at one point featured over seven hundred locations, including up to six in the Circle City. The chain proved popular until 1968, when it was sold by the original owners. A series of ownership changes in the 1970s doomed things for the Dog. Many locations ceased the branding, instead opting to go independent. Examples of this in Indianapolis included Bill's Fabulous Fifties on Rockville Road and the Suds in Greenwood. A Lafayette businessman by the name of Donald Van Dame, along with a Dallas investor, purchased the rights in 1991 and began expanding heavily in the Indianapolis market. The expansion proved too rapid, and the company was in trouble by 2002. Most stores were converted to Sonic Drive-Ins. The rights to the company were kept and licensed to around six operators in Indiana and Illinois. Fortunately, a terrifically preserved Dog 'n' Suds continues to operate along the Sagamore Parkway in Lafayette, Indiana. *Courtesy of Jeff Kamm.*

the Mai-Tai. Tom would see the evolution of the Keystone store over the next twenty years. By the 1990s, Knobby's had undertaken a retro diner–like existence. Regular customers would flock for its famous roast beef and catfish dinners. Daily specials such as ham and beans and fish sandwiches added some extra flair to the menu. Featuring waitresses who served as original carhops in the 1950s, the restaurant stood as a pillar of familiarity to local diners, some of whom sought out heaping piles of comfort food daily.

Keystone Avenue has been one of the busiest commuter avenues in the city for decades. By 2001, British Petroleum was looking to make a big splash in the local gasoline market and set its sights on the popular but aging restaurant. Tom Knoll closed the landmark in 2001, after receiving an offer he couldn't refuse. The BP station remains on the site to this day. The unique-looking Mai-Tai operated through the 1980s as Mac's Restaurant and then converted to a karate studio. The long-vacant building remains standing—barely—to this day as a final monument to a longtime Indianapolis tradition.

AFTERTHOUGHT

Indianapolis has seen monumental growth throughout the years. What was once a sleepy state capital that awoke to the world one weekend every May now stands out as a dynamic and cosmopolitan city. In 1960, the entire metropolitan area consisted of Marion County, which had a population of just under 700,000. These days, the city serves as the hub to a metropolitan region that consists of eleven counties and a population estimated at over 2 million souls. One can see this in the number of restaurants. *Polk's City Directory* of 1961 listed a grand total of just under five hundred restaurants. According to phone listings and Yelp Reviews, the number of restaurants now exceeds four thousand. There are definitely many more options for hungry Hoosiers today. Unfortunately, this explosion has often come in the form of chain restaurants. It's hard to blame folks for drifting toward consistency and familiarity, but this comes at a cost to the charm and uniqueness of the city. One common gripe among the owners of the few legacy restaurants that remain is the competition from these corporately backed behemoths that enjoy the advantages of product distribution and nationally backed advertising campaigns. Fortunately, tastes seem to be changing. Although the Meridian Street strip is a shell of its former glory of the 1950s and '60s, new entertainment districts are flourishing along Massachusetts Avenue, Virginia Avenue and, more recently, East Sixteenth Street. The vast majority of these newly sprung dining spots and watering holes are fiercely independent, offering unique tastes oftentimes crafted by local products.

Despite the city's evolution from a sleepy crossroads jokingly referred to as "Naptown" into a thriving metropolis, a great sense of nostalgia exists among longtime residents. Many different discussion groups have popped up on social media with the purpose of remembering many long-gone places and people. When researching for Historicindianapolis.com and this book, much attention was paid to those restaurants that were most talked about had the biggest impact on people's lives. The focus was primarily on local, independent restaurants.

There have been notable chains. Burger Chef comes to mind. The fast-food giant, founded in 1954, once was second only to McDonald's in number of locations across the United States. The chain's salad days were in the 1960s and '70s, and its legacy is entrenched in pop culture. It recently was a topic on the popular AMC series *Mad Men*. The chain lost steam after changes in ownership and disappeared in the early 1980s after being purchased by the parent company of Hardee's. It is greatly missed. Several books and websites are dedicated to the memory of this home-grown eatery.

Although originally established in Illinois, the Steak 'n' Shake chain of restaurants has long been associated with Indianapolis. What began as a Midwest chain of drive-in restaurants has grown to well over five hundred locations throughout the South, Northeast and Southwest. The company has been headquartered in Indianapolis since it was purchased by Indiana University graduate Ed Kelley in the early 1980s. Kelley was responsible for much of the chain's growth during the 1980s and '90s. Now under the stewardship of Sardar Biglari, the chain recently relocated its corporate headquarters to a restored downtown building.

There have been many other examples of much-loved chains that have come and gone. Victoria Station carved prime rib in a series of salvaged box cars on both the north and south sides. Howard Johnson's served up its signature fried clams and twenty-eight flavors of ice cream under a beckoning orange roof on all corners of the city until the mid-1980s. Cincinnati-based Frisch's Big Boy has had a love-hate relationship with the city, arriving in the 1950s only to disappear entirely in the 1960s, with another return in the '80s followed by yet another retreat. The company recently announced that a third attempt will be made to lure in Indianapolis diners with its iconic roadside statuary. Other long-gone fast-food outlets include Arthur Treacher's Fish and Chips, Shakey's Pizza, Rax Roast Beef and Dog 'n' Suds drive-ins.

While it's fun to reminisce about what has been lost over the years, it is also important to support what we have. Be sure and visit one of our longtime favorites on a more frequent basis. Make it a point to try a new, independent eatery on your weekly date night. Supporting these institutions will ensure our uniqueness and help shed that ugly "Naptown" image for good. Bon appetit!

Appendix

SELECTED RECIPES

Although many of the establishments discussed are long gone and the remaining ones keep their secrets closely guarded, here are some recipes that may be of note for those wanting to re-create some of their favorite meals at home.

BREADED PORK TENDERLOIN

The staple of any good 1950s era drive-in is the breaded pork tenderloin. The origins of this Hoosier tradition are unclear; however, it appears to be a variation of schnitzel, which would have been popular with the sea of German immigrants. It became a running gag for many drive-ins to pound the meat so thin that the shear circumference of the meat dwarfed the miniscule bun. Sandwiches are traditionally served deluxe, topped with lettuce, tomato, onions, pickles and mayonnaise or ketchup. Despite the immense popularity in Indiana, the sandwich is scarcely found outside the state's borders. Here is a recipe for those wayward Hoosiers.

¾–1 pound pork tenderloin
2 eggs
4 teaspoons water
½ teaspoon salt
¼ teaspoon dried rosemary, crushed (I use LOTS more)
1 dash pepper
¾ cup dried breadcrumbs
3 tablespoons vegetable oil

Cut pork tenderloin into ½-inch slices. Pound to about ¼-inch thickness. In a pie plate or medium bowl, beat egg with water, salt, rosemary and pepper. Place breadcrumbs on wax paper. With tongs, dip meat into egg mixture to coat both sides, roll in breadcrumbs and fry until golden—about 5 minutes a side.

L.S. AYRES'S CHICKEN VELVET SOUP

6 tablespoons butter
6 tablespoons all-purpose flour
½ cup milk
½ cup light cream
3 cups chicken broth
1 cup cooked chicken, finely chopped
Dash of pepper

Melt butter in a saucepan. Blend in flour and then stir in milk, light cream and chicken broth. Cook over medium heat, stirring constantly until mixture thickens and comes to a boil. Reduce heat. Stir in finely chopped chicken and pepper. Return soup to boiling and serve immediately. Makes about 5 cups.

SHRIMP COCKTAIL SAUCE

Every steakhouse in Indianapolis seems to be in competition these days for who has the best shrimp cocktail. This friendly rivalry was started by the legendary St. Elmo's steakhouse. The fiery prawns are legendary and often featured in promos during televised events in the city. Here is a recipe for a sauce that one might encounter at one of the area steakhouses.

5 tablespoons fresh horseradish.
½ cup cider vinegar
2 cups bottled chili sauce
Squirt of lemon juice

Soak the fresh horseradish in the vinegar for 1 hour. Drain the horseradish and mix with the chili sauce. Add lemon juice. Serve with chilled cocktail shrimp with the tails still attached.

TEEPEE SALAD

One of the most famous aspects of the Teepee Drive-In was its unique salad. It featured chopped lettuce served with the salad dressing below, topped with julienne-cut beats. This recipe should be pared down, as most folks aren't in need of gallons of dressing—unless expecting the whole tribe.

GARLIC OIL:
3 whole bulbs (not cloves) garlic
1 gallon of salad oil
14 ounces paprika
6 ounces seasoned salt
4 ounces sugar
3 ounces salt
1 full mayonnaise recipe (see below)
1 tube anchovy paste
14 ounces wine vinegar
1 quart water

Peel garlic and add to salad oil. Let garlic soak overnight in the oil. Stir together paprika, seasoned salt, sugar and salt and add to mayonnaise, along with anchovy paste. Add 10 ounces of the garlic oil (save the remaining oil for other recipes), then add vinegar and water and stir thoroughly. Makes 3½ to 4 gallons.

MAYONNAISE:
13 ounces sugar
6 ounces salt
2 ounces dry mustard
½ ounce nutmeg
½ ounce ginger
½ ounce paprika
½ ounce white pepper
18 eggs
2 gallons salad oil
4 quarts water
2 pounds cornstarch
8 ounces cider vinegar

Stir together sugar, salt, dry mustard, nutmeg, ginger, paprika and white pepper and set aside. Beat eggs well with mixer on high speed, and slowly add salad oil. Bring 3 quarts of water to a boil. Mix each pound of cornstarch with a ½ quart of remaining water until smooth. This prevents the mixture from being lumpy. Add the cornstarch/water mixture to boiling water, stirring constantly to keep smooth. Cook mixture until it is nice and thick. Add cornstarch mixture to egg and salad oil mixture and stir well. Add dry mixture, and then add cider vinegar and mix thoroughly. Makes 3 gallons.

TEMPURA-FRIED CARROTS

Although long gone, Macri's Italian Garden was a longtime favorite Indianapolis dining destination. Although not a traditional Italian dish, one of the most talked-about items were the unique fried carrots. Regulars describe them as being breaded in a light tempura batter. Here is a recipe for vegetable tempura that you can use at home to try and re-create this missed delicacy.

Peanut oil (or canola)
6 cups rice flour
1 tablespoon annatto (optional)
1 tablespoon chili powder (optional)
1 quart chilled club soda
Carrots, cut julienne style

Heat the oil in a deep fryer or cast-iron skillet, bringing it to 360°F.

Make the Batter: In a medium mixing bowl, add the rice flour and seasonings (optional). Next, add the club soda, ensuring that it is cold before mixing. You're looking for the consistency of pancake batter. It should be loose enough to coat things easily but not drip off. If the batter is too thick, add club soda or ice water 1 tablespoon at a time until it loosens. If too thin, add rice flour 1 tablespoon at a time until it comes together. Make sure to mix thoroughly so there are no lumps.

Coat the Carrots: The carrots can be tossed in the batter bowl ahead of time and allowed to sink a little to coat each stick. This will be easier and less messy than hand dipping. Toss items in and help them sink or roll to be coated with batter.

Fry the Vegetables: Next, lift carrots out of the batter with a slotted spoon and allow them to drain. Drop the carrot pieces, in small batches, into the oil one at a time, ensuring they don't touch. Most everything will immediately sink to the bottom. Use a strainer or long-handled utensil to loosen them and keep them moving. This will allow them to cook evenly on all sides. Cook the carrots for 4 minutes. Make sure you allow the oil to return to temperature before starting a new batch.

Remove from Oil: Remove your freshly fried carrots from the oil with a spider or the basket the unit comes with. Place them on a few layers of paper towels to allow remaining oil to drain. Give them a light sprinkling of salt and allow to cool slightly.

BIBLIOGRAPHY

Indiana State Library, Indianapolis Newspaper Collections

Indianapolis News, October 2, 1967; January 20, 1970.

Indianapolis Star, April 16, 1940; December 21, 1940; September 26, 1952; February 3, 1954; November 13, 1955; October 1, 1957; May 17, 1958; March 7, 1959; June 16, 1963; June 21, 1964; August 21, 1964; October 18, 1964; November 3, 1964; December 5, 1964; January 19, 1965; February 28, 1965; August 3, 1966; September 8, 1966; November 12, 1967; November 16, 1968; November 1, 1970; February 23, 1973; May 25, 1973; April 26, 1975; April 25, 1978; June 12, 1978; September 9, 1979; September 20, 1979; October 13, 1979; November 24, 1979; November 23, 1980; November 1, 1981; December 1, 1982; March 27, 1983; October 16, 1983; Special Feature, 1984; January 2, 1986; June 19, 1987; October 23, 1987; May 15, 1988; November 9, 1990; October 26, 1991; December 31, 1991; October 4, 1994; February 3, 1996; March 30, 1996; April 11, 1996; April 12, 1996; May 20, 1997; August 6, 2000; August 3, 2001; March 22, 2002; June 6, 2002; May 8, 2003; October 16, 2003; February 17, 2004; May 27, 2004; July 5, 2006; December 9, 2009; June 4, 2013; June 11, 2014.

Other Print Sources

The Encyclopedia of Indianapolis. Indianapolis: Indiana University Press, 1994.
Indianapolis Business Journal, August 5, 1991.
Indianapolis Convention and Travel Guide. Indianapolis: American National, 1978.
Indianapolis Monthly (August 1994, August 1997, November 1997, September 2002 and May 2007).
Indianapolis Yellow Pages, 1987.
New Faces at the Crossroads. Indianapolis: Indiana University Press, 2007.
Nuvo Newsweekly, November 2011.
Polk's City Directory, 1989.
Polk's Indianapolis City Directory, 1945, 1959, 1960, 1964, 1966, 1970, 1978, 1985, 1987.
Reid Duffy's Guide to Indiana's Favorite Restaurants. Indianapolis: Indiana University Press, 2006.
Southside Voice, October 21, 2015.
Temple, Mary Beth. *Driving the National Road in Indiana.* Pamphlet, 2006.
Turchi, Kenneth. *L.S. Ayres and Company: The Store at the Crossroads of America.* N.p., 2012.

Web Sources

http://dicksummer.com/dsblog/the-dick-summer-re-connection-chapter-14/#more-18
http://lanifogblog.blogspot.com/2007/02/jong-mea-restaurant.html
http://milanoinn.com/about-milano-inn
http://restaurant-ingthroughhistory.com/recipes
http://www.cooks.com/recipe/ph6f26uz/tee-pee-salad-dressing.html
http://www.harryandizzys.com/our-story
http://www.steerin.net
http://www.stelmos.com/wp-content/uploads/2013/01/StElmo-History-2011.pdf
http://www.thekitchn.com

INDEX

ABOUT THE AUTHOR

Indiana native Jeffrey S. Kamm is operations manager at the International Center in Indianapolis and a contributor to the website HistoricIndianapolis.com. He writes a weekly column for the site, "At Your Leisure," that focuses on historic restaurants, hotels, theaters, artistic organizations and sport franchises. Jeff has worked in the hotel industry and earned a BS in hospitality and tourism management from Purdue University.